Teaching Around the 4MAT® Cycle

Teaching Around the 4MAT® Cycle

Designing Instruction for Diverse Learners With Diverse Learning Styles

Bernice McCarthy   Dennis McCarthy

Foreword by Gordon Cawelti

CORWIN PRESS
A SAGE Publications Company
Thousand Oaks, California

For information:

Corwin Press
A Sage Publications Company
2455 Teller Road
Thousand Oaks, California 91320
www.corwinpress.com

Sage Publications Ltd.
1 Oliver's Yard
55 City Road
London EC1Y 1SP
United Kingdom

Sage Publications India Pvt. Ltd.
B-42, Panchsheel Enclave
Post Box 4109
New Delhi 110 017 India

Printed in the United States of America.

Library of Congress Cataloging-in-Publication Data

McCarthy, Bernice.
Teaching around the 4MAT® cycle: Designing instruction for diverse learners with diverse learning styles / Bernice McCarthy, Dennis McCarthy.
    p. cm.
Includes bibliographical references and index.
ISBN 978-1-4129-2529-7 (cloth) — ISBN 978-1-4129-2530-3 (pbk.)
   1. 4MAT system. 2. Learning. 3. Left and right (Psychology) 4. Learning, Psychology of.
I. Title: Teaching around the 4MAT cycle. II. McCarthy, Dennis, 1961- III. Title.
LB1029.A13M34 2006
371.39—dc22   2005018388

This book is printed on acid-free paper.

09   10   11   12   9 8 7 6 5 4 3

Acquisitions Editor:	Faye Zucker
Editorial Assistant:	Gem Rabanera
Production Editor:	Diane S. Foster
Copy Editor:	Barbara Ray
Typesetter:	C&M Digitals (P) Ltd.
Proofreader:	Mary Meagher
Indexer:	Molly Hall
Cover Designer:	Rose Storey
Cover & Text Illustrator:	Margaret Gray Hudson
Graphic Designer:	Lisa Miller

Contents

Foreword

The press for teachers to help all of today's diverse learners attain high standards has never been higher, but today's legislation may also produce a citizenry more adept at rote learning than the true conceptual understanding required to deal with complex issues. Such side effects of educational policies were not intended but may already be counter-productive for students seeking to further their academic careers or to enter the work world where higher order thinking is required.

The highly important life work of Bernice McCarthy, which continues in this new book, represents one of the very few well thought out and researched-based approaches to teaching and learning. Teachers can rely upon the strategies in this book to ensure that the diverse students they face each day will be provided with a challenging set of learning experiences that will serve them well in the future.

We have long known that good teaching begins when we present students with a problem, issue, or phenomenon as we try to raise their interest in the topic at hand. This is critical in the discovery method in science and was a first stage of Madeline Hunter's now famous formulations about teaching. This posing of an issue to be questioned and understood begins McCarthy's 4MAT cycle, and teachers are given plenty of assistance here in helping students see what the issue is and why it should be understood.

Brain-based research also has shown us that students must be given an opportunity to think about such issues or problems as they attempt to formulate a tentative hypothesis for or explanation of the phenomenon in question. This is the next important phase of 4MAT, and it energizes the thinking processes that are underemphasized in the "drill and kill" exercises common in too many classrooms where the pressure is on to improve test scores rather than to teach.

Students will welcome the planned activities as the next feature of well designed lessons, and teachers are offered substantial suggestions for incorporating these activities into daily classroom events designed to help students prove their hunches or begin to seek alternative explanations. This phase is as important today as when John Dewey emphasized "learning by doing" a century ago when schools sought to be more instrumental in preparing students for a fuller civic life.

The remaining phase of the 4MAT cycle helps teachers see how to lead students into making application of their new knowledge and skills—in other words, to see how to make use of what they have learned.

Teachers using the McCarthy approach can be helped to far better lesson-planning skills than many now have, and when this becomes automatically a part of their daily instructional life their students will surely benefit. *Teaching Around the 4MAT Cycle* represents a well conceived developmental use of the extensive research on brain-based teaching methods.

Teachers and administrators need to ensure that the pressure for teaching to standards does not have the regression effect of moving backward in what we know about addressing the needs of diverse learners. The approach advanced in this important book helps make sure that when it comes to education, the teaching profession is heard as well as the politicians.

—Gordon Cawelti
Educational Research Service, Arlington, VA

Prologue

S ince 1979, we have been teaching teachers to more effectively connect with learners using a method of instruction called 4MAT. 4MAT describes a cycle of learning that begins by engaging learners through direct experience and then moves them toward reflective observation (1), followed by abstract conceptualizing (2), active experimentation and problem solving (3), and finally toward integration of new content and skills (4) and readiness to begin the cycle anew (1).

This book summarizes the basic elements of 4MAT. It begins in Chapter 1 with a discussion of learning style and the ramifications of this research for teachers and learners. Chapter 2 moves beyond learning style to describe a cycle of learning that appeals to all types of learners in turn. In Chapter 3, we offer practical advice for teachers on applying the learning cycle to the classroom.

Chapter 4 presents practical application of the latest brain research, suggesting that teachers use multiple methods in terms of both the delivery of new material and student expressions of understanding. In Chapter 5, we combine the notions of learning style, the cycle, and brain research to present the complete 4MAT model.

Concepts are a key element in engaging learners using 4MAT. Chapter 6 offers guidance on understanding and delivering the bigger picture in the classroom. Last, in the final chapter, we offer a template for unit planning with 4MAT that brings it all together—the cycle, learning style, brain research, and concept-based teaching.

Since 1979, 4MAT has helped hundreds of thousands of teachers connect to learners. We sincerely hope this material will strengthen that connection for you. This book offers a summary of the research and ideas comprising the 4MAT System. Feel free to visit www.aboutlearning.com for detailed information on companion materials and teacher training.

—*Bernice McCarthy and Dennis McCarthy*

About the Authors

Bernice McCarthy and **Dennis McCarthy** are founding members of **About Learning, Inc.,** which is a training, consulting, and publishing company that helps organizations improve the quality of their learning programs by teaching them to design more effective learning systems. About Learning works with schools and school districts as well as with private and public sector organizations to discover what it takes for people to learn well and to offer turnkey instructional programs in key content areas that reflect sound educational theory and practice. About Learning offers books, software, training programs, and training design consultation to a wide range of organizations to assist them in designing more effective training or instructional programs.

Acknowledgments

Publisher's Acknowledgments

Corwin Press and the authors acknowledge with gratitude the in-depth reviews and insightful comments of the following reviewers:

Julia Koble, NBCT, Biology Department Head and About Learning Consultant, Minot High School, Minot, ND

Robert Sylwester, Emeritus Professor of Education, University of Oregon, Eugene, OR

We also acknowledge the following reviewers for their contributions:

J. Kay Giles, Superintendent, Prairie Hills ESD 144, IL

Robin Kvalo, Principal, Rusch Elementary, Portage, WI

Max McGee, Superintendent, Wilmette District 39, IL

Fred Morton, Superintendent, Montgomery County Public Schools, Christianburg, VA

Patricia Shelton, Director of Certification and Professional Development, Brevard County Schools, FL

1

Learning Styles

What follows in this chapter is a study of learning style theory, the rationale underlying the choices learners make along the continua of perceiving and processing.

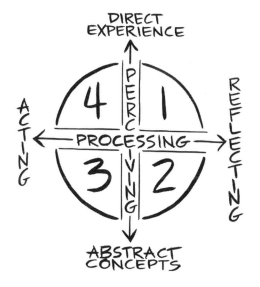

A CYCLE OF LEARNING

Learning styles are the result of preferences in the ways people perceive and process experience. They are described in a four-quadrant construct. But learning styles are not the most important thing; by themselves, they offer no guidance for teachers. For this guidance, we turn to the cycle of learning.

This cycle is defined by the four axes. Picture a clock. At 12:00 we have the top of the perceiving line. This place on the cycle represents direct experience, the feeling place. At 6:00, at the bottom of the perceiving line, we have abstract concepts, the thinking place. Twelve o'clock is subject, being "in it." Six o'clock is object, "studying it."

The two points of the processing line represent a move from reflection (at 3:00) to action (at 9:00).

Now put the whole clock together. Learning begins with direct experience at 12:00. Then learners move toward analysis at 6:00 via reflective processing at 3:00. After the cycle swings past 6:00, learners become more active, moving from analysis to usefulness via active processing at 9:00. The movement from 9:00 back to 12:00 offers learners the opportunity to integrate the new material back with the self. Learning is complete at the top of the cycle.

Learning style. Particular approaches individuals have to perceiving and processing information and experience that result in certain preferred places on the learning cycle, to the partial exclusion of others.

While relatively stable over time, our style preferences are highly affected by the situations we find ourselves in. We do what we have to do. But some of those situations are a real stretch.

It is critical that we learn to be flexible at those places on the cycle that are a challenge for us, even as we maintain our individual learning preferences—the special spins we put on our growth and development. Teachers must design instruction with a framework that encompasses the cycle and honors individual differences throughout the complete learning process.

HOW PERCEIVING DEFINES US AS LEARNERS

HOW WE PERCEIVE

We perceive things differently. We take things in differently. In new learning situations, some of us sense and feel our way, staying with our direct experiences. Others think things through, preferring to move quickly to abstractions.

Those who perceive in a feeling way, an intuitive way, sense the experience, connecting the information to meaning. They learn through the lens of the affect, the emotional. These sensor-feelers believe in their intuition. They are, by their very nature, holistic. The gestalt of direct experience at 12:00 is home to them.

On the other hand, those who think through their experiences tend more to the abstract. They analyze what is happening, examining the parts. Their intellect makes the first appraisal. They reason experience.

Analysis necessitates a standing outside, an attempt to override (although never entirely possible) the personality of the perceiver. This is the 6:00 place where learners strive to be as free from bias as possible.

"Who could ever tire of this heart-stopping transition, of this breakthrough shift between seeing and knowing you see, between being and knowing you be? It drives you to a life of concentration, it does, a life in which effort draws you down so very deep that when you surface you twist up exhilarated with a yelp and a gasp."[1]

The particular perceiving orientation that you come to favor over time, feeling (depending largely on direct experience) or thinking (depending largely on abstraction), is one of two major factors determining who you are as a learner. Both kinds of perception are equally valuable; both have their own strengths and weaknesses.

Schools do not value the feeling approach; it is grossly neglected (and even that is an understatement). Progression through the grades leads learners away from feeling, dealing more and more with abstractions about experience—botany without flowers, astronomy without stars, life skills without emotion. This is very frustrating for those who are feelers, and a great loss for those who are thinkers as well.

I do in fact doubt that schooling, as presently conceived and conducted, is capable of providing large segments of young people with the education they and democracy require, and I include among these young people a significant proportion of those now "making it."

—John Goodlad

HOW PROCESSING DEFINES US AS LEARNERS

The second major difference in how we learn is how we process what we experience, what we *do* with what happens to us.

Some of us jump right in and try things; others watch what happens and reflect on it before jumping in. Some of us reflect; some of us act. Both approaches have their strengths and weaknesses.

Schools ask learners to watch and listen and reflect. This is frustrating for those who need to act, to do, to try things. (This is a great loss for those who prefer to reflect, as well.) Those who prefer to reflect filter new learnings through their own experiences.

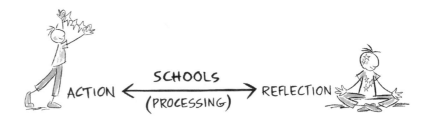

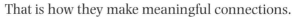

That is how they make meaningful connections.

Those who prefer to act need to try things out; they need to *do it*, to extend it into their world. That is how they make meaningful connections.

Even if the theory that now exists were perfect, most of us in education have never before worked from theory to practice. . . . We cannot expect the theory itself to solve our problems. The understanding has to be applied.

Deciding what is to be abandoned is crucial . . . and letting go is often much harder than taking hold.

—Leslie Hart

THE PROCESSING DIMENSION AND JOHN DEWEY

John Dewey maintained that if learning is real, it will create purpose and direction. That direction will lead to change and then to transformation.

Dewey talked of the transaction between the learner and the environment. His theory of education is a theory of doing. Dewey addressed the importance of human experience as the gateway to understanding.

Cognitive potential evolves through use. Learning happens as we unite our experiences and their meaning with actions that test those meanings in the world. Dewey believed we should unite mind and body through a method of thinking and doing he called "the art of education."

Schools have overlooked the wisdom of Dewey. Think of how different our assessment strategies would be if we applied Dewey. For example, students would have performance requirements. They would have to do what they learn. It would not be enough to recite information. Learners would have to make what they learn useful. They would have to show how they use it in their lives.

All children have intelligence. We have asked the wrong question. We ask, "How much?" We must ask, "What kind?"

—Mary Meeker

PERCEIVING AND PROCESSING AND STYLE

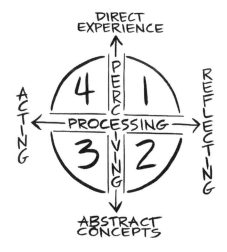

Our favorite places on the 4MAT cycle result in individual learner differences. The perceiving continuum of 4MAT moves from direct experience (DE) to abstract conceptualizing (AC). Those of us who feel more graceful in direct experience tend to linger at 12:00. Those of us who feel more graceful in conceptual abstraction tend to linger at 6:00.

The processing continuum of 4MAT moves from reflection (R) to action (A). Those of us who feel more graceful in reflection tend to linger at 3:00. Those who feel more graceful in action tend to rush toward 9:00.

The combination of these two choices forms our individual differences. I call them:

Type one learners,

Type two learners,

Type three learners, and

Type four learners.

Designers of instruction at all levels, in all fields, in all settings both formal and informal, need to understand the legitimacy of these differences and design instruction to accommodate them.

Type One Learners: Why?

Type one learners perceive information directly at 12:00 and process it reflectively at 3:00.

They learn by feeling their experiences, being present to them, trusting in their perceptions, and being open to sensory input. They take time to reflect and ponder their experience. They seek meaning and clarity. They integrate experience with the self. They learn primarily in dialogue, by listening and sharing ideas. They excel in viewing these ideas from many perspectives. They have highly developed imaginations. They are insightful, absorbing reality, taking in the climate. They thrive on lots of reflecting time, especially when pondering new ideas. They seek commitment. They work for harmony and clue in to the needs of others with ease. They are great mentors. They nurture others to help them accomplish their goals. They tackle problems by reflecting alone and then brainstorming with others. They exercise authority through group participation. If they are forced into a conflict situation (which is usually difficult for them), they deal with it through dialogue and a great deal of listening. They build trust through personal interactions.

Their favorite question is "Why?" They seek to know the underlying values.
As teachers they:

Are interested in facilitating individual growth and self-awareness,

Encourage their students to be authentic,

Believe curricula should help students know themselves and others,

See knowledge as the basis for achieving potential,

Involve their students in discussions and group projects,

Believe reflection is a primary method for enhancing self-awareness, and

Are informed about social issues that affect human development.

Strengths: People skills, reflection

Goals: To be involved in important issues and to bring harmony

Need to Improve: Working under pressure and taking risks

Type Two Learners: What?

Type two learners perceive information abstractly at 6:00 and process it reflectively at 3:00.

They learn by thinking through experiences, judging the accuracy of what they encounter, examining details and specifics. They take the time to reflect and ponder on what they experience. They seek to achieve goals and to be personally effective. They integrate their observations into what they already know, forming theories and concepts. They excel in traditional learning environments and are thorough and industrious. They judge new learning by how theoretically sound it is. They are intrigued by how systems function. They look for structure. They thrive on stimulating lectures and readings. They seek continuity and certainty and are wary of subjective judgments. They have clearly defined goals and monitor cutting-edge research in their fields. They want to be as knowledgeable and accurate as possible. They are systematic. They tackle problems with logic and analysis. They exercise authority with principles and procedures. If they are forced into a conflict situation, they deal with it systematically, dissecting the problem before coming to a conclusion. They build trust by knowing the facts and presenting them systematically.

Their favorite question is "What?" They seek to know what the experts know. As teachers they:

Are interested in transmitting the best knowledge,

Try to help their students become good thinkers,

Encourage excellence,

Believe curricula should encompass significant information with facts in service to that goal,

See knowledge as the basis for achieving goals,

Involve their students in lectures, note taking, and readings,

Believe people should approach learning systematically, and

Are up-to-date on the expert knowledge in their content areas.

Strengths: Concepts and theory, reflection

Goals: Intellectual recognition

Need to Improve: Creativity

Type Three Learners: How Does This Work?

Type three learners perceive information abstractly at 6:00 and process it actively at 9:00.
They learn by thinking through their experiences, judging the usefulness of what they encounter. They take the time to figure out what can be done with what they learn. They seek utility and results. They integrate new learning by testing theories. They excel at down-to-earth problem solving, often tinkering to make things work.

Type three learners learn best with hands-on techniques. And once they have it, they move quickly to mastery. They are pragmatists; they need closure; they like to get things done. They thrive in the company of competent people and excel at problem solving. They seek to get to the heart of things. They work for deadlines and "keep to the plan." They like to be considered competent, and they help others to be competent. They tackle problems quickly, often without consulting others. They exercise authority with reward and punishment. If they are forced into a conflict situation, they deal with it by creating solutions. They build trust with straightforward forcefulness.

Their favorite question is "How does this work?" They seek to know the usability of theory.

As teachers they:

Are interested in helping their students achieve high skills competence,

Try to lead their students to mastery for life skills,

Encourage the practical aspects of learning,

Believe curricula should stress economic usefulness and opportunity,

See knowledge as enabling learners to make their way in the world,

Involve their students in problem solving, experiments, and hands-on activities,

Believe their students should approach problems scientifically, and

Excel in the technical aspects of their fields.

Strengths: Action, getting things done

Goals: Productivity, competence

Need to Improve: People skills

Type Four Learners: What If?

Type four learners perceive information directly at 12:00 and process it actively at 9:00.

They learn from their perceptions and the results of their experiences. They are open to all manner of sensory input. They take the time to consider the possibilities of what they learn. They seek challenge and are risk takers. They integrate their present experiences with future opportunities. They learn primarily through self-discovery. They excel at synthesizing. They are flexible and flourish in challenging situations. They are enthusiastic about enriching reality, putting new "spins" on things. They thrive on chaotic situations. They seek to influence others. They push their potential. They are at ease with all types of people. They actively seek growth and pressure others to do so. They tackle problems with their intuition. They exercise authority by influence and expect their people to be accountable. If they are forced into a conflict situation, they react emotionally and then move to cool rationality. They build trust with high communication skills and openness.

Their favorite question is "What If?" They seek to know the possibilities.

As teachers they:

Are interested in enabling learners to seek possibilities,

Help their students act on their dreams,

Believe self-awareness comes from challenging oneself,

Encourage real-experience learning,

Believe curricula should be geared to individual learner interests,

See knowledge as important to bringing about change,

Involve their students in many out-of-school activities, and

Use the community as their classroom, seeing community needs as learning opportunities.

Strengths: Innovation and action for change

Goals: To be on the cutting edge of social progress

Need to Improve: Digging into the details

Putting It All Together

Learning moves from 12:00—the sensory place, the "Me" place, where we feel our world—from direct experience (DE) into reflective observation (RO). Then we assimilate the experience and abstract it into a concept (AC).

We stand back and examine; we name "It." The 6:00 place is the "It" place, where things are objects to be examined and understood. Then we try things out, discovering what personal meaning we can make of this experience, this thing, transforming concepts into actions via active experimentation (AE).

Last, we return to new direct experience (DE) with an ever-renewing focus. We have integrated meaning, concept, and action.

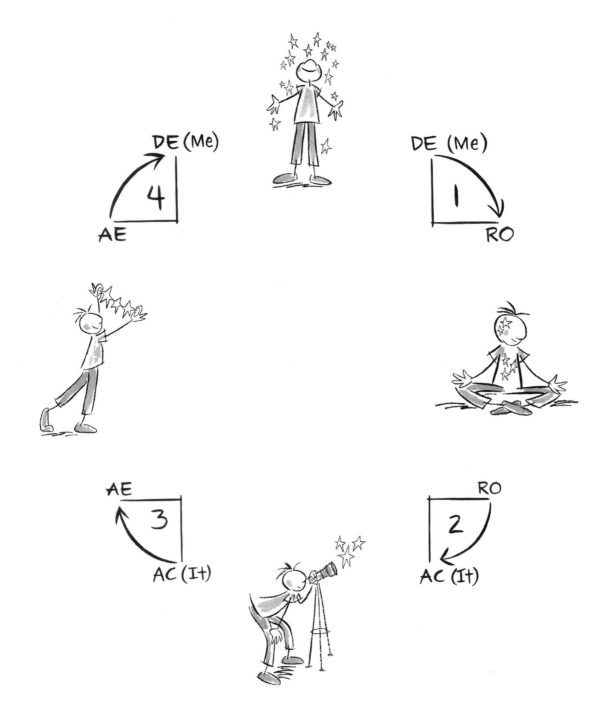

NOTE

1. Dillard 1974.

2

A Cycle of Learning

MOVING AROUND THE CYCLE

The movement around the 4MAT cycle represents the learning process itself.

It is a movement from experiencing,

to reflecting,

to conceptualizing,

to tinkering and problem solving,

to integrating new learning with the self.

It is a movement that involves a constant balancing and rebalancing between being in experience and standing apart to analyze that experience,

between subjective and objective,

between connected and separate,

between being and knowing.

From connectedness to separation, back to connectedness. From "in here" to "out there."

First We Experience

When we experience something new, we are initially immersed in it because when we are drawn to something, we approach it with our whole selves. We are subjective, biased, and inclined with certain leanings about it. We are subject to it, both

EXPERIENCE

apprehending it and captured by it. We are embedded in it. At this point in the learning we are embedduals: caught in the web of our own meaning.

Then We Reflect

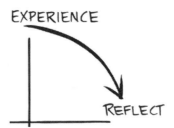

Almost immediately we begin the process of filtering the experience. We filter it from behind our own eyes, through who and what we are, and to where our past has brought us at this particular moment. We internalize newness through our subjective feeling filter. We experience newness in the schemata of our personal world.

As we begin this filtering process, we emerge from our embeddedness in the newness and separate from it. We release our subjectivity in our need to become objective.

Then We Conceptualize

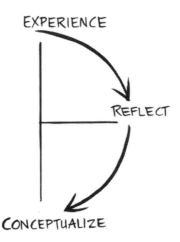

We stand back, examine, narrow our focus. We name it, conceptualize it, attempt to understand it. We move to comprehension. We move to objectivity, to abstract conceptualization, to the cognitive. We move from percept to concept. This separation is necessary to truly see the newness. Our inner feeling appraises where we are with this new thing, then our cognitive examines. We are interested, curious, intrigued.

We separate ourselves from it. We symbolize it by naming it. We look at what others—our peers, the experts—say about it; what others have done with it; where it fits into the scheme of the larger world. We move to comprehend it, to have it, not to be had by it.

Then We Act

Comprehension, however, is not enough. We must try it, tinker with it, play with it, watch it, and make it work. We must do it. Now that it has become the object, we become the object manipulator. We interact with it, we use it, we see how it works for us—first the way others do it, then in our own way.

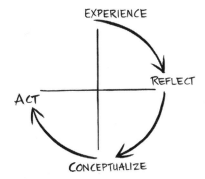

Finally, We Integrate

We change it to suit us; we enrich it. We place it in our world; we transfer it to where we live. We adapt it, making something new of it. We integrate it. We are enriched by it. And we are transformed.

Then, and only then, learning has happened. Learning doesn't happen until 11:59! This making of meaning, which is learning itself, is in and out, into the self and out to the world, over and over again. We need to relate anew continuously to make meaning.

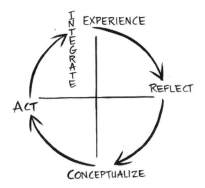

This adaptive conversation is the very source of, and the unifying content for, thought and feeling . . . this process is about the development of knowing.

—Robert Kegan

THE CYCLE BEGINS AND ENDS WITH THE INDIVIDUAL

All learning begins with the self. The cycle moves from personal connections at 12:00, to the knowledge of the experts at 6:00, and back to the self as the learning is personally adapted. This process transforms the learner through new understanding and skills.

The cycle is a movement from subject to object to integration, which is a powerful definition of learning. Moving around the cycle takes us from being subjective (embedded in the experience) to standing outside the experience and examining it as an object (becoming objective).

If we stay in tune with this movement of meaning, the conversation that unifies feeling and thought continues. We connect, we separate, and we connect anew. We try what we have understood by acting on our conclusions, then moving back to deeper integration each time.

This returns us to experience again. The conversation goes on. Feeling and thought interact and merge the possibilities for newness and continuous learning without limit. Learners move from subjectivity, to objectivity, to integration—the complete learning act.

The oneness of the overall system is paramount.

—David Bohm

ANY SUCCESSFULLY COMPLETED CYCLE WILL FLOW TO REFLECTION ON ITSELF

If a cycle is completed with meaning and attention, students will naturally reflect on the entire experience. This reflection on past cycles follows whenever deep and important learning happens. Teachers need to build in reflection time and reflective activities for their learners, both during and after the cycle.

The Cycle Is a Consummate Design for Curriculum

Successive cycles extend not only to the next lesson or unit but also all the way through the curriculum. I know of no better way to structure curriculum. The cycle is useful not only for individual units but also for designing frameworks for entire programs: kindergarten through Grade 12, college, adulthood, corporate training. The 4MAT cycle ensures conceptually coherent and balanced instruction and appeals to the legitimate diversity of all learners.

The Cycle Encompasses
Important Assessment Benchmarks

The cycle frames assessment in a manageable way. Assessment is not just facts, recall. But how to master the techniques that might bring comprehensive assessment programs to our learners is not well understood, let alone practiced to any degree in our schools. We must assess meaning connections, along with verbal and nonverbal representations of concepts. We must measure how knowledge is connected and understood relationally. We need strategies that measure our ultimate purpose in teaching and training, which is performance. Both curriculum and assessment issues are discussed at length in Chapter 6.

Renew thyself completely each day, do it again, and again,
and forever again.

—Chinese inscription

THE CYCLE IS A
SHOWPLACE FOR DIFFERENT
STYLES AT DIFFERENT PLACES

Each of us shines at different places on the cycle based on our preferences. Certain places on the cycle are simply more comfortable for us than others. When we are in our comfortable place, we are graceful and sure of ourselves; we feel at home. These places are very different for different learners.

That is why teams composed of diverse learners who trust one another are successful. Their different gifts combine to form a rich and successful complexity.

THE CYCLE IS A STRETCH
FOR ALL WHO TRAVEL IT

This is true because we are comfortable in some places but challenged in others. Mastering the entire cycle is a stretch, but well worth the effort.

THE CYCLE IS A FORMULA
FOR HUMAN GROWTH

We are here to make meaning, and this cycle frames that process.

THINK ABOUT YOURSELF

Work Task: Where are you on the learning cycle?

In an average day of 16 hours (eight hours for sleeping):

How much time do you spend experiencing the now, what is actually happening in the moment?

How much time do you spend reflecting on what has happened?

How much time do you spend thinking, examining, focusing on some aspect of what interests you intellectually?

How much time do you spend acting, doing the things your day demands of you?

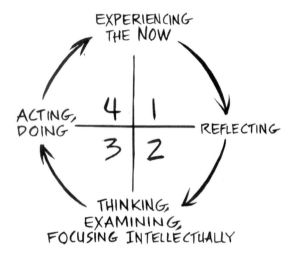

Which parts of the cycle are your strengths?

OTHER WAYS TO LOOK AT THE QUADRANTS

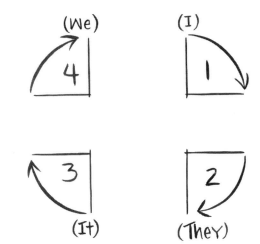

Try looking at the four quadrants from another perspective. Think about Quadrant One as the place for "I." The activities you create as a teacher will all tend to impact the "I" of your students; that is, their own personal place.

☆ How might you create strategies in each part of the cycle looking at it from this perspective?

My "I" activities in Quadrant One

My "They" activities in Quadrant Two

My "It" activities in Quadrant Three

My "We" activities in Quadrant Four

The "I" of Quadrant One

Something is happening to the person's feelings. The teacher has connected the activity that is happening to the students' past experiences. Responses are: "I know how that feels" or "I have been there myself."

The focus is not on the teacher. The focus is on the student connecting, the student remembering, the student resonating. It is not a telling time; it is a feeling, dialogue (sharing) time. And it is "I" all the way.

Often teachers can even add to the discussion after it gets going and model the "I" part of their past experiences along with the students, so long as it does not take away from the student dialogue.

The "They" of Quadrant Two

The experts are the "They." As well, the data—the facts and information—are all "They."

This is the listening time, and the clearer the expert knowledge is—the more it is fashioned to suit the backgrounds and levels of the students—the better it is received.

Master teachers make sure all the students get it. They tell it in multiple ways, they make it available in some form to be checked later by those who need to return to it in their own time, and they use visual as well as verbal forms to aid understanding.

The "It" of Quadrant Three

The "It" is concrete. It is something to have in the hand, meaning it is something one must do. It is other than the student; it is an object to be mastered, to be done, to be experimented with, to be practiced.

Practice should be multiple. Most of all, however, practice should be structured. The students must follow a series of steps that lead them to fluid expertise so at some future point they will be able to discard the steps. The teacher's goal is to lead students to personal expertise that is useful to them for the rest of their lives. (How does memorizing the 50 state capitals of the United States fit into this definition of learning?)

The "We" of Quadrant Four

The purpose of Quadrant Four is to have students adapt learning to their world and to use it to influence their future. The emphasis is on the "We" because students are extending themselves, empowered with new learning, out into a wider dialogue. Now the student has a more powerful voice.

☆ Try this perspective with one of your lessons. Put it on this wheel and then examine it for I, They, It, and We.

YET ANOTHER WAY TO LOOK AT THE QUADRANTS

Try the inside/outside perspective.

Quadrants One and Two are inside—known from within.

Quadrants Three and Four are outside—known from without.

Looking at the outside, Looking at the inside

HONORING

How can they
now interact
with their
world?

extension

How will they
master this
learning?

What happens
inside them?

intention

What happens
to their
thinking?

Looking at the Outside   **Looking at the Inside**

Discovering my new
power or lack of it

My perception

Interacting with the world

How it shakes out
with others

Speaking in my
own voice extended

Discovering my reactions

Learning from my doing

Reliving my experiences

Finding new questions

Hearing my inner voice

Learning how others do it

Data

Learning it their way

Knowledge

Seeing what happens to it

Expert views

Examining the reactions

Becoming skilled with it

Enhancing or
critiquing my beliefs

Ask yourself these questions regarding one of your own lessons:

How can they now interact with their world?

What happens inside them?

How will they master this learning?

What happens to their thinking?

3

Teaching
Around the Cycle

The 4MAT cycle begins with being and moves to thinking. A lesson unit must begin with being. It must begin where your students are.

This chapter describes each progressive phase of the 4MAT framework and how to create lessons that move through all four quadrants. The 4MAT cycle requires that teachers establish their conceptual goals, create classroom climates that are conducive to honoring diversity, set up essential questions that go to the heart of the concepts, and create a total learning cycle complete with multiple kinds of assessments.

QUADRANT ONE:
ANSWERING THE "WHY?" QUESTION

You open the learning process in Quadrant One, bounded by the parameters of direct experience at 12:00 and reflective observation at 3:00.

Oneness: What Your Students Will Experience

☆ Personal, meaningful connections based on experience

☆ Sharing storytelling to correlate meaning

☆ Engaging in dialogue (no telling in Quadrant One, please), initiating conversations about the possible meaning of the material

☆ Seeing the material in context with some bigger idea or picture

☆ Establishing relationships

☆ Listening and sharing similar experiences

☆ Speaking with subjective voices

☆ Experiencing camaraderie, having a sense of "having been there, too"

☆ Experiencing the diversity of how others see things

☆ Gaining insights into their own experiences through that of others

☆ Creating high interest in the material to come

☆ Establishing resonance

☆ Becoming aware of the value of learning

☆ Experiencing the discrepancies that learning will unravel

☆ Focusing on present and past understandings

☆ Creating a sense of "I know something about this, and I want to know more"

The climate is one of trust and openness, with permission and encouragement to explore diverse meanings. The method is discussion of experiences. The students engage in collaborative learning, each contributing their individuality. The teacher initiates, motivates, and creates experiences that capture the students and strengthen student collaboration.

Dialogue is at the root of the learning process.

—Asa Hilliard

Your teaching task in Quadrant One is to engage students in an experience that will lead them to value and pursue the learning you initiate. Get them to see how the material will connect to their lives.

Learning is not rote; it is how we make meaning. It is directly related to how we feel about what we learn. When we talk about successful learning, we are talking about feeling, answering the "Why?" questions:

"Why do I need to know this?"

"Why is this material valuable in my life?"

"Is there a larger context?"

Answer these questions by making connections with your opening activity. For example, how would you address the "Why?" when teaching fractions to a fifth grade class? Would your answer be "Because it is in the fifth grade math book," or "Because it will be on the achievement test," or "Because the state standards say I have to teach fractions in the fifth grade"? All of those reasons have some validity, but they are not objectives for your students. Why do children need to learn fractions? Because they can use them. When they understand that we can look at sections of things in order to comprehend the wholeness of things, when they understand that we can manipulate parts to rearrange wholes, when they understand that some things can be understood discretely, then they will see the importance of "fractionness."

In other words, the content you teach must carry its own "Why?" and its own benefit aside from the school's reasons. Your students must see the validity of the content for themselves, or you will struggle to keep them focused and attentive.

> *What is a humanizing relationship? One that reflects the qualities of kindness, mercy, consideration, tenderness, love, concern, compassion, cooperation, responsiveness and friendship. Education needs to focus on human interaction.*
>
> —David and Roger Johnson

Use your content knowledge to create a Quadrant One experience that will lead your students to want to learn, to become fascinated by learning. In the case of fractions, you would set up a situation in which they come to value what fractions are and want to manipulate them for themselves—not for the school's sake and not just to do well on an achievement test.

If you do not create a motivational Quadrant One, little learning will follow. Get your students' attention. Make your content come alive. "Attention is the most basic form of love."[1] Get your students to attend; get them to love the learning!

Work Task Quadrant One Questions: Establishing the "Why?"

> *Learning is the making of meaning.*
>
> —Robert Kegan

> *The kind of learning that should occur stems from the kinds of questions asked.*
>
> *They should be questions that raise issues, questions that lead to further questions.*
>
> *Seldom questions are answered with a simple yes or no.*
>
> —The Paideia Group

1. Do you introduce your subject by setting up situations that learners can recognize, beginning by building on what they already know?

(5) All the time   **(4) Quite often**   **(3) Sometimes**   **(2) A little**   **(1) Not at all**

_____✓_____   _____   _____   _____   _____

2. Do you set up situations that draw out learners' subjective comments (personal past experiences and feelings) about the material to be learned?

(5) All the time   **(4) Quite often**   **(3) Sometimes**   **(2) A little**   **(1) Not at all**

_____   _____✓_____   _____   _____   _____

3. How often do you construct actual experiences in which your students are involved in an event, rather than merely reading information or asking students to listen to someone give them information?

(5) All the time   **(4) Quite often**   **(3) Sometimes**   **(2) A little**   **(1) Not at all**

_____   _____   _____✓_____   _____   _____

4. How often do you present a problem that contains within it a hint of the discrepancies that the learning will resolve?

(5) All the time   **(4) Quite often**   **(3) Sometimes**   **(2) A little**   **(1) Not at all**

_____   _____   _____   _____✓_____   _____

5. How often do you lead your learners into discussions with their fellow students, encouraging them to share personal experiences that will help them understand the value of the learning that is about to take place?

(5) All the time   **(4) Quite often**   **(3) Sometimes**   **(2) A little**   **(1) Not at all**

_____   _____✓_____   _____   _____   _____

Enter the sum of your responses to the Quadrant One questions. _18_____

QUADRANT TWO: ANSWERING THE "WHAT?" QUESTION

In Quadrant Two, you move learners from experiencing to conceptualizing through reflection, bounded by the parameters of reflective observation at three o' clock and abstract conceptualization at 6:00.

The question you focus on in Quadrant Two is "What?"

What do my students need to know to master this content?

What are the essence pieces, the core concepts that will lead them to understand more with less?

What parts of this content do I need to emphasize so they will understand it at this core level?

Twoness: What the Students Experience in Quadrant Two

☆ Connecting fascination to facts

☆ Comprehending the learning

☆ Receiving expert knowledge

☆ Examining pertinent information with the most salient facts

☆ Establishing links between subjective experience and objective knowing

☆ Seeing both the big picture and the supporting details

☆ Organizing

☆ Connecting to other similar ideas

☆ Classifying

☆ Comparing

☆ Blending personal experiences with expert knowing

☆ Patterning

☆ Clarifying purpose

☆ Bringing out the structure, the form

☆ Theorizing

☆ Engaging in interactive questioning

☆ Focusing on current hypotheses

☆ Creating knowledge that will give a solid ground to further understanding

The climate is one of receptiveness, taking in, being briefed, a thoughtful, reflective ambiance of attuned and active listening.

The method is information delivery through lecture, readings, and demonstrations to examine expert findings. In Quadrant Two, learners cross a bridge from the world of the self to the world of the experts.

Students bring their experiences in Quadrant One with them to Quadrant Two. Those experiences are processed further in some nonverbal way before the content delivery begins.

The teacher creates this bridge with a nonverbal task and then delivers the content, thus melding student experience with expert knowledge.

*We cannot even begin to say
what an intelligence is
until we first ascertain
what kinds of knowledge
are available to it.*

—Jeremy Campbell

For the information delivery part of the cycle, all manner of delivery works: demonstrations, videos, the Web, film, satellite conferencing, etc.—anywhere pertinent and current knowledge and information are available.

The teacher moves the learners to objectivity, teaching them to stand aside and examine the concept the way the experts see it, detailing the facts and discerning the underlying theory. This foundation prepares them for the next step, the mastery of the skills.

Work Task Quadrant Two Questions: Establishing the "What?"

*A formal and orderly conception of the whole is
rarely present.*

—Barnard

*Belief and understanding are not enough.
It has to be done.*

—Wayne Dyer

1. Do you present the material you teach in broad strokes, determining the key pieces that form the essence, so your students can sense the simplicity underlying the complex?

(5) All the time   **(4) Quite often**   **(3) Sometimes**   **(2) A little**   **(1) Not at all**

_____   _____   ✓ _____   _____   _____

2. Do you emphasize essential rationales, focusing on understanding and seldom asking for rule memorization?

(5) All the time   **(4) Quite often**   **(3) Sometimes**   **(2) A little**   **(1) Not at all**

_____   _____   ✓ _____   _____   _____

3. Do you require that learners explore the relationships among various sections of your material?

(5) All the time   **(4) Quite often**   **(3) Sometimes**   **(2) A little**   **(1) Not at all**

_____   ✓ _____   _____   _____   _____

4. Do you ask your students to synthesize as well as analyze? Do you keep these two in balance?

(5) All the time   **(4) Quite often**   **(3) Sometimes**   **(2) A little**   **(1) Not at all**

_____   _____   ✓ _____   _____   _____

5. Do you keep returning to the major concepts as you move through the various parts of your instruction?

(5) All the time   **(4) Quite often**   **(3) Sometimes**   **(2) A little**   **(1) Not at all**

✓ _____   _____   _____   _____   _____

Enter the sum of your responses to the Quadrant Two questions. __18__

QUADRANT THREE: ANSWERING THE "HOW?" QUESTION

In this quadrant, bounded by the parameters of abstract conceptualization at 6:00 and active experimentation at 9:00, learners move from expert knowledge into personal skill and usefulness, the beginning of the return back to themselves. The question you focus on in Quadrant Three is "How?"

How will my students use this in their real lives (not just their school lives)?

How will this content affect their power?

Knowledge is the most powerful problem-solving tool there is. If I want to solve problems in mathematics, I must have mathematical concepts. However, there is a difference between teaching knowledge as a tool that facilitates problem solving and teaching it simply as a thing to be memorized.

Threeness: What Your Students Experience in Quadrant Three

☆ Learning important skills

☆ Practicing

☆ Experimenting

☆ Using expert knowledge to get something done

☆ Testing accuracy

☆ Doing

☆ Establishing the link between theory and application

☆ Seeing how things work

☆ Predicting

☆ Recording the details in action, not just in theory

☆ Questioning

☆ Comparing results

☆ Seeing how form operates

☆ Resolving discrepancies

☆ Reaching conclusions

☆ Mastering skills

☆ Extending the learning into usefulness in real life

The climate is active. Teachers offer opportunities for students to tinker, try things out, to begin to become experts themselves.

The method is working in centers, with partners and in teams (or alone for some students), experimenting, tinkering, practicing.

The teacher is the coach, facilitating, nurturing experiments, guiding the questioning, providing adequate practice for mastery.

The key to Quadrant Three is letting students discover how valid the learning is for them. Require mastery, that they use the learning in their own lives. This is where the learning really begins.

> *Along the path of learning,*
> *playfulness is the thing.*
>
> —Unknown

> *My chief want in life*
> *is someone who*
> *shall make me do*
> *what I can.*
>
> —Ralph Waldo Emerson

Teachers who need control seldom go past the 6:00 place on the 4MAT cycle. They stay in Quadrant Two, where they surround themselves with the safety of the experts. They deliver content, initiate practice routines, and move on to deliver more content. Our textbooks are constructed this way. They prefer to tell and have their students tell back, with little or no change in the telling. This is not learning!

"Nothing takes root in mind when there is no balance between receiving and doing."[2]

Learning is becoming more—more skillful, more knowledgeable, more skeptical, more capable, more interested in one's own growth.

Learning is never just the test results. It must be used.

Let the material be changed by the student as the students are changed by the material.

Learning is a conversation.

Work Task Quadrant Three Questions: Establishing the "How?"

> *If it is not used, it is not learned.*
>
> —Luria

1. Do your practice activities emerge from both the main concepts and the factual data?

(5) All the time   (4) Quite often   (3) Sometimes   (2) A little   (1) Not at all

_____ ✓_____ _____ _____ _____

2. Are there elements of play and wonder in the hands-on activities that you require?

(5) All the time   (4) Quite often   (3) Sometimes   (2) A little   (1) Not at all

_____ _____ _____ _____ ✓_____

3. Do you set up opportunities to learn by doing: field-based experiences, information searches beyond the classroom, experiments, and tinkering possibilities?

(5) All the time   (4) Quite often   (3) Sometimes   (2) A little   (1) Not at all

_____ _____ _____ ✓_____ _____

4. Do you require that your students test or check out the information they are learning?

(5) All the time   (4) Quite often   (3) Sometimes   (2) A little   (1) Not at all

_____ _____ _____ _____ ✓_____

5. Do you set up situations that call for hunches concerning possible outcomes?

(5) All the time   (4) Quite often   (3) Sometimes   (2) A little   (1) Not at all

_____ _____ _____ ✓_____ _____

Enter the sum of your responses to the Quadrant Three questions. _10_____

QUADRANT FOUR: ANSWERING THE "IF?" QUESTION

In this quadrant, bounded by the parameters of active experimentation and direct experience, learners complete the movement back to themselves. They refine their use of what they have learned, integrating it into their lives.

The question the teacher focuses on in Quadrant Four is "If?" If my students master this learning, what will they be able to do that they cannot do now? What power will they have attained as persons? If they learn this, what new questions will they have?

Fourness: What Your Students Experience in Quadrant Four

☆ Adapting the learning

☆ Modifying

☆ Reworking

☆ Verifying usefulness

☆ Summarizing

☆ Creating new questions

☆ Breaking boundaries

☆ Synthesizing

☆ Establishing future use

☆ Refocusing

☆ Editing and refining

☆ Confirming conclusions

☆ Taking a position

☆ Creating new discrepancies

☆ Making new connections

☆ Evaluating

☆ Exhibiting, publishing

☆ Re-presenting

☆ Performing

☆ Celebrating

☆ Sharing the learning

The teacher creates a climate of celebration, one that is performance-oriented . . . a sharing place with results that can be measured, with new and better questions, with growth.

The method is mentoring, creating resources, and enhancing self-discovery, assisting learners as they adapt and create their own usefulness.

The teacher is the cheerleader, facilitating independence, getting resources, championing, and leading students to meticulous self-evaluation.

The key to Quadrant Four is the adaptation. It is what the learners make of the learning and how they use it in their lives. This is the creative manifestation of the learning. It is the learning activated, behaviorized. It is what Elliot Eisner speaks of when he says learners need to become "idiosyncratic gourmets," putting their individual "spins" on the learning.[3]

Multiple alternative assessments are necessary here to cover the range of unique outcomes inherent in this kind of instruction. Performance assessment requires a specific listing of criteria for evaluation. Students need to know what is expected of

them and how they will be measured when they are asked to perform what they are learning, as opposed to merely reiterating what they have been told.

Because each of us is unique, the choices we make to use what we learn lead us back to ourselves. This is how it should be.

Throughout the cycle, the teacher stresses the personal meaning of the learning, first motivating, then informing, then guiding practice, and finally encouraging the imaginative usefulness of performance. Educators should dedicate their lives to increasing their students' abilities to master their own destinies.

> *Keep an eye out*
> *for the tinker shuffle,*
> *the flying of kites,*
> *and kindred sources of surprised amusement.*

> —Unknown

Work Task Quadrant Four Questions:
Establishing the "What If?"

> *The act of creating is the act of the whole person.*

> —Bruner

1. Do you often discuss the value of making a difference in the world with your students?

(5) All the time   **(4) Quite often**   **(3) Sometimes**   **(2) A little**   **(1) Not at all**

_____   ____✓_____   _____   _____   _____

2. Do you give multiple opportunities for your learners to prove mastery?

(5) All the time   **(4) Quite often**   **(3) Sometimes**   **(2) A little**   **(1) Not at all**

_____   _____   _____✓_____   _____   _____

3. Do you engage your learners in open-ended problem solving in which the solutions are multiple?

(5) All the time   **(4) Quite often**   **(3) Sometimes**   **(2) A little**   **(1) Not at all**

_____   _____   _____✓_____   _____   _____

4. Do you encourage your students to add their own innovations to the requirements of your courses?

(5) All the time   **(4) Quite often**   **(3) Sometimes**   **(2) A little**   **(1) Not at all**

_____   _____   _____   _____✓_____   _____

5. Do you use rubrics (specified assessment criteria) that are understood and agreed on up front? Do you ask students to help you construct those rubrics?

(5) All the time   **(4) Quite often**   **(3) Sometimes**   **(2) A little**   **(1) Not at all**

_____   _____✓_____   _____   _____   _____

Enter the sum of your responses to the Quadrant Four questions. _16_

PLOT YOUR QUADRANT TEACHING SCORE

Directions: Plot the four sums from the previous pages on the diagonal lines inside the quadrant. Then connect the dots to see a picture of your teaching tendencies within the 4MAT quadrants.

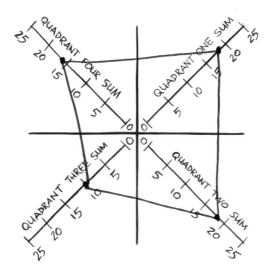

A NOTE ON THE CYCLE

If you successfully guide your learners through this cycle, you will have accomplished something very real. All your students will experience learning. They will experience comfort, and they will be required to stretch. Such is all learning: There are places where we are graceful and places where we stumble. The stumbling places offer opportunity for growth.

Learners will be drawn into the learning. They will examine and experiment with significant concepts. They will integrate the learning into their lives, which will draw them to further learning opportunities.

Through all of it, we must learn how to learn. And so the cycle repeats, at higher and higher levels.

NOTES

1. Tarrant 1998.
2. Dewey 1934.
3. Eisner 2004.

4

The Brain–Mind Learning System

The effects of genetic and environmental factors are inextricably mingled from the earliest stages of development. The remarkable combination of gene-controlled factors, some of them conserved for over a billion years, together with an enormous range of idiosyncratic factors, both internal and external, help account for the uniqueness of each individual.

—Opening remarks at the 4th Symposium
on the Human Brain, Arnold B. Scheibel, MD,
University of California, Berkeley, March 1998

There is one key question to answer when we combine the findings on style with the brain research: **Can we design an instructional system that capitalizes on all the phases of the learning act, honoring the diversity of our students and using the best and most brain compatible techniques?**

To explore this question, we must look further at the complexity of human beings. We need to understand something about the uniqueness each person brings to the learning act in light of the current brain research. Examining this research can help teachers accommodate learner diversity with instruction that appeals to both left- and right-mode processing. This section addresses the brain throughout the learning act, from emotion and its impact on memory, to reasoning, to tinkering, to adapting and creating.

People don't come preassembled, but are glued together by life.

—Joseph LeDoux

SOME IMPORTANT DEFINITIONS

Brain: The major organ of the nervous system.

Cognitive neuroscience: A loose federation of philosophy, psychology, and biology.

Emotion: A brain representation of changes in body states connected to particular mental images that activate a specific brain system. It is an unconscious arousal system that leads the way to all learning. Emotion in the brain produces feelings in the body. Emotions are public; by and large people can observe one another's emotions. There is no single place in the brain for processing emotion.

Feeling: A representation of the changes in an organism induced by an emotional response. Feeling can be both conscious and unconscious. Damasio (1999) claims, "There is no central feeling state before the respective emotion occurs." And he makes a further major point: "I am suggesting that having a feeling is not the same as knowing a feeling, and reflecting on a feeling is yet another step up." Feelings are private.

Core consciousness: A sense of self about the present, the here and now.

Extended consciousness: A complex phenomena that evolves across a lifetime creating an autobiographical self. Working memory is vital for this process.

Consciousness is constructing knowledge about two facts. The first is the organism, the "me"; the second is the object that the "me" is encountering. This encounter creates a relationship that has a transforming effect on the organism, a relationship between the two.

Image: A mental pattern in any of the sensory modalities.

Thinking: Organizing and manipulating new information with previous information in order to understand something. There is a major interaction between feeling and thinking.

I have tried many times
to think of cognitive tasks
that do not involve feelings.
So far I have failed.

—James E. Zull

LINEAR AND ROUND PROCESSING

Current research indicates that mapping a "geography" of the brain, that is, limiting certain functions to locations in the brain, is inconsistent with current brain findings.

What we once referred to as left- and right-mode are more dynamic and interactive than previously understood and are better served with the terms "linear" for left-mode and "round" for right-mode. What remains clear is that optimal problem solving is achieved through a dynamic balance of the two.

Why should any map be skewed to one hemisphere rather than being bilateral? Damasio (1999) comments, "In humans as well as nonhuman species, functions seem to be apportioned asymmetrically to the cerebral hemispheres, probably because one final controller is better than two when it comes to choosing an action or a thought." Siegel (1999) reports that the separation between the two hemispheres can be very "independent at times and directly shapes the construction of subjective experiences." And Robert Sylwester says, "We have learned and continue to learn much about the duality of the hemispheres. It is not a static structure, it is a continuing, dynamic system" (R. Sylwester, personal communication, February 2005).

According to Elkhonon Goldberg's research (2001) on the frontal lobes, "Novelty and familiarity are the defining characteristics in the mental life of any creature capable of learning." He asks, "Is it possible that the existence of two different, separate but interconnected systems, one for novelty and the other for routines, facilitates learning?" Goldberg believes that it is, and that the exploratory behavior in novel situations is the domain of the right hemisphere (what I am now labeling "round") and the cognitive routines the domain of the left ("linear").

Goldberg's findings have major ramifications for teachers. If, as he claims, novelty is the chief domain of the right hemisphere, then beginning a unit with a lecture, delivered in a linear, verbal fashion, does not strike me as the proper way to introduce new learning. The presenter would have to be capable of high emotional appeal as well as be skilled in the content knowledge and its immediate connections to his or her particular students.

Much I reflect on the good and the true
In the faiths beneath the sun
But most upon Allah Who gave me
Two
Sides to my head, not one.
I would go without shirt or shoe,
Friend, tobacco or bread,
Sooner than lose for a minute the two
Separate sides of my head!

—Rudyard Kipling

THE FOUR QUADRANTS AND THE BRAIN

4MAT adds the processing preferences of the two hemispheres, linear and round, to each of the four quadrants on the 4MAT cycle. That is not the only brain connection, however. The movement from perceiving to reflecting to conceptualizing to adapting that encompasses the way the brain works takes place throughout the cycle.

4MAT asks teachers to include in all important learning:

Concrete experiencing: Sensing direct physical information from both the world and our bodies, which creates images in our brain directly related to those experiences.

Reflecting: Connecting and integrating past experiences, including images.

Conceptualizing abstractions: Symbolizing, comparing, contrasting.

Actively experimenting: Connecting abstractions to actions: intellectual, hands-on, communication, performance, and back to more complex and higher-level experiences.

Contrast this cycle with Damasio's (1999) list of how we come to know: "From observer, to perceiver, to knower, to thinker and then to actor."

And Zull's (2002) comments on the cycle and its relationship to the brain:

> The functions of the cerebral cortex are sensing, integrating and generating action. This is the natural learning cycle.

We believe that 4MAT's very foundation is brain-based, and, given that our mission is to help people learn, our students must learn to routinely use all the parts of the cycle.

Neuroscience has illuminated the duality. Education has attempted to apply it. But the right mode remains elusive. It is not easy to describe in words. It is difficult to communicate the understanding of the right mode, simply because of the ineffable qualities of insight and intuition. The receptivity of the senses, the suspension of analysis, the quest for meaning are difficult to illuminate in precise language.

> The greater the fluency in nonverbal thought, the greater the dysfluency in verbal communication.[1]

Individuals differ regarding these two methods of approaching learning. The American poet Robert Frost puts it this way:

> Scholars get their knowledge with conscientious thoroughness along projected lines of logic; poets theirs cavalierly and as it happens . . . snatching a thing from some previous order with not so much as a ligature clinging to it of the old place where it was organic. [2]

We need to help our students see things with the mind's eye, visualizing how the parts make up the whole, excelling in spatial skills. We need to help them see concepts in pictures and use these images to create metaphors that form new combinations of ideas, enabling insight leaps to sudden new knowing.

We need to help them to relate disparate parts, to synthesize. To combine the best of both processing modes is to bring learners to excellence:

The complexity of percept and concept,

understandings of both heart and head.

Analysis and synthesis,

being and knowing integrated.

Consider a consummate musical performance. Imagine the result when performers play with the highest technical expertise while pouring their souls into the music, which in turn resonates in the souls of the audience.

Or recall chaos theory, in which the shape informs the system, in which the ability to see spatially combines with the ability to master system thinking. As James Gleick explained:

Linking topology and dynamical systems is the possibility of using a shape to help visualize the whole range of behaviors of a system. Bending the shape a little corresponds to changing the system parameters. . . Shapes that look roughly the same give roughly the same kinds of behavior. If you can visualize the shape, you can understand the system.[3]

Capitalize on both modes of learning. This is high-powered understanding. Expertise with details maximizes the power of corresponding visual representations. The ability to use both processing modes skillfully needs to be a major goal of all instruction.

Frank Benson, an important writer on creativity, characterizes the ability to form concepts as

bihemispheric, the right mode forming the visual image, the left, the semantic relationship. The combination produces a total concept.[4]

The brain is a dynamic structure that employs both modes in a marvelously complex interplay, and its highest action is to unite the processing of the two modes.

The goal of education is to develop the flexible use of both of these processing modes, instructing and encouraging students to use their whole brain systems by allowing time for

Lecturing and interacting,

Naming and picturing,

Demonstrating and letting them do it,

Following a sequence to check on a known reaction and tinkering in a self-discovery mode, and

Answering queries and creating new questions.

What follows is a list of teaching strategies that we believe are brain-compatible; that is, they impact learning in multiple ways. Their use covers a wide range of learning inducers that appeal to the amazing human brain and help it thrive.

> *But there is also the athlete, who can carry the whole game in his head—the racing car driver who can visualize an entire race. Such intuitive models have played a major role in the history of human survival, and an important part of this intelligence is the ability to build accurate models of reality in one's mind.*
>
> —Thomas West

Linear Processing

Examines cause and effect

Breaks things down into parts, examines and categorizes

Seeks and uses language and symbols (The structure of the English language promotes and reinforces linear strategies.)

Seeks theory, creates models

Is sequential, works in time (Time is the quintessential characteristic of linear processing.)

Some key words to remember:

parts, categories, cause and effect, grids, sequence, words, next

Linear processing is interested in knowing those things that we can describe with precision, classifying, discriminating, and naming.

It is . . .

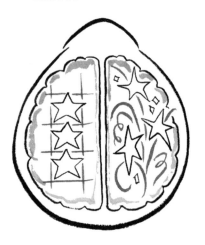

A technical text

When the statistics confirm

Great verbal directions

Hearing exactly what was said

Edges

Time

Nouns

Text (as opposed to context)

An explainer

Round Processing

Intuits feeling states

Understands and honors wordlessness

Sees wholes, forms images, mental combinations

Seeks relationships, discrepancies, connections

Functions visuospatially—manipulating forms, distances, space

Is simultaneous

Some key words to remember:

wholes, images, relationships, discrepancies, simultaneity, insights, subjectivity, nonverbal

Round processing perceives the world how it is. Round processing knows more than it can tell, filling gaps, thinking aside, imaging.

It is . . .

Storytelling

Musical moments

Body language and tone of voice

Centers, nubs

"In the zone"

Poetry, painting with words

Verbs

Context rather than text

Seeing things as they are; explanations actually disrupt this sight.

Some learners who are at ease in round processing have trouble describing what they think. The imagery of poetry suits them better, in which words become holograms and metaphors connect and explain. They struggle with words to express what they understand. They know more than they can tell.

Others learners are at ease with the linear. They describe what they mean with precision (and are proud that they can do so). They are frustrated with ambiguity and roundness. They seek to specify, to account for, to make distinctions.

Both kinds of learners need to enhance their gifts. Both need to be honored for being who they are and for what they bring. Teachers need to develop instructional methods that teach in and to both modes. The goal of education needs to be whole-brain flexibility, encouraging divergent and convergent thinking, merged with the theoretical and the intuitive and presented with conceptual rigor.

Well-functioning adults reveal a coordinated functioning of both hemispheres. Elkhonon Goldberg (2001) suggests that the right hemisphere is important for processing novelty and the left for processing cognitive routines, a dynamic, gradual shift from right (round) to left (linear).

Examine the following continua in light of Goldberg's contention. For example:

Round: knows the world through images (pictures)

Linear: knows the world through symbols (words)

Does this make sense, that the round right would lead to the left linear, which then routinizes the learning? It makes all kinds of sense to us.

Linear	*Round*

Knowing

Knows the world through symbols	Knows the world through images
Is rational	Has intuitive insights
Has a drive to explain, to create	Sees things as they are, with little interpretations and conclusions alternation
Looks at the parts	Looks at the whole
Engages in if–then thinking	Networks
Produces coherences, shuts down	Questions threatening facts

Language

Negotiates an external world of symbols	Negotiates with images, body symbols, sensations
Uses verbal information	Uses nonverbal information
Is efficient at processing routine	Is efficient at processing novel codes, situations
Cues in on the literal	Cues in on the unspoken
Is into grammar and syntax	Is into nuances, inflections

Music

Strengths are duration, temporal	Strengths are tone, timbres, order, rhythm melodies
Left ear (right side) responds more to music	Right ear (left side) responds more to speech

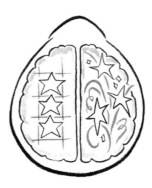

Memory

Remembers names and sequences   Remembers events and places

It is indisputable that there are two profoundly different modes in which the mind processes information. One or the other mode can dominate our conscious experience at various times.

—Frank Benson

You've got to get all of the combinations out of your head, so you can look at the whole structure, go beyond it. Good representation is a release from intellectual bondage.

—Jerome Bruner

Any experiences that help develop the processing abilities of both hemispheres will improve individuals' internal and interpersonal lives.

STUDENT LEARNING STRATEGY PREFERENCES

Those Who Favor Linear Processing

Prefer verbal instructions

Like controlled, systematic experiments

Prefer problem solving with logic

Find differences

Like structured climates

Prefer established information

Rely heavily on the verbal

Like discrete information recall

Control feelings

Are intrigued with theory

Excel in propositional language

Draw on previously accumulated information

Seek routines, familiarity

In subtle ways individuals tend to gravitate toward one or the other approach to life.

—Elkhonon Goldberg

Those Who Favor Round Processing

Prefer demonstrated instructions

Like open-ended experiments

Prefer problem solving with hunching

Find similarities

Like fluid and spontaneous climates

Prefer elusive, ambiguous information

Rely on the nonverbal

Like narratives

Are more free with feelings

Need experiences

Excel in poetic, metaphoric language

Draw on unbounded qualitative patterns, clustering around images

Seek novelty

Uniting the activities of the two hemispheres is the highest and most elaborate activity of the brain.

—Richard Restak

LINEAR PROCESSING WORDS

Sometimes, determining whether an activity is right mode or left can be as simple as looking at the key words. Here is a partial list of words that are considered left mode. Circle the ones that are most prevalent in your teaching.

observe	research	uncover contradictions	revise
discuss	compare	collect	refine
diverge	contrast	inquire	produce evidence
develop coherence	plan	predict	verify
conceptualize	theorize	record	summarize
define	outline	hypothesize	assess
classify	test	measure	evaluate
discriminate	verify	manage	come to closure
acquire knowledge	analyze	order	refocus
tell	write analytically	select	produce
listen	reason	flowchart	take a position
sit still	identify	write an essay	conclude
read	break into parts	edit	form new questions
view	drill		

ROUND PROCESSING WORDS

Circle the ones that you use most.

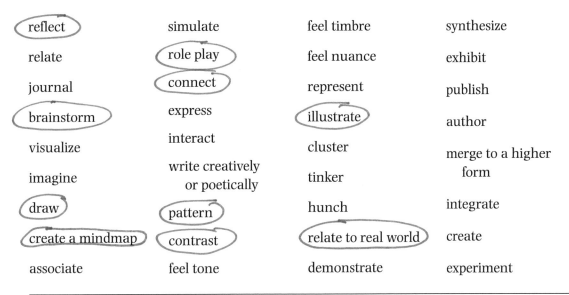

reflect

relate

journal

brainstorm

visualize

imagine

draw

create a mindmap

associate

simulate

role play

connect

express

interact

write creatively
or poetically

pattern

contrast

feel tone

feel timbre

feel nuance

represent

illustrate

cluster

tinker

hunch

relate to real world

demonstrate

synthesize

exhibit

publish

author

merge to a higher
form

integrate

create

experiment

TEACHING STRATEGIES
THAT FAVOR THE WHOLE BRAIN

The mind is profound and complex, responding to challenges, developing routines, enhancing expertise with those routines, and moving on to ever-new challenges. Yet, we remain anchored in instruction that is designed for

uniformity,

control of inputs and behavior,

confirmation of the teacher's/instructor's knowledge,

repetition of activities and information, and

linearity, in thinking and in sequencing.

This is incompatible with how the brain works!

On the next pages, we invite you to examine some strategies that favor brain-compatible teaching.

Using Metaphors and Similes

Using metaphors may be one of the most rewarding round activities because of the possible payoff. When we create a metaphor, we must understand the core of something in order to contrast it with something else. Try answering these yourself:

How is a tree like a poem?

What metaphor will describe best for you the meaning of an algorithm?

Creating metaphors reveals the essence of material. For example, What is the heart of the meaning of Huck Finn? How is photosynthesis like feeding your dog?

Patterning

Find patterns in ideas, texts, and manner of visuals—a look at the whole to discern similarities and repetitions. Encourage your students to see the discrepancies in patterns as well.

EXAMPLE: Create a record of how you spend your time, when you get home from school until you go to bed, for five school nights. Describe any pattern you see, comment on how happy you are with what you see, and suggest possible options for what you might want to change.

Using Imagery

Create pictures of concepts, relationships, and connections. Put thoughts into three-dimensional space to better understand associations, links, and overall coherence. Figurative language provides intensity as well as clarification; it helps to illuminate an idea, to forge comparisons.

EXAMPLE: Depict the essay you wrote on justice, the police, and teenagers with images you believe explain your thinking and your feelings on the subject. You may use magazine images or your own original ones. Be sure your feelings are clear to the observer of your work.

Raising Sensory Awareness

Use techniques that call on auditory, visual, kinesthetic, tactile, and olfactory senses as a key to more enriched understanding and to add perspective from different angles

EXAMPLE: Think of music that sounds like joy, or melancholy, or triumph. Explain what makes it so. Or, dance the meaning of startling change. Or, tell me what anger smells like. Or, create a texture that feels like competition.

Poetic Language

All the uses of poetic language—metrics, the way a line breathes, pattern and sound merging, balance and design, rhyme and energy—can be used to create images that tell so much more than does mere literal text. Poetic language can be used in many more content areas than one would think. It is a truly fine match to some areas of mathematics, for instance. It can be an excellent technique for aiding understanding, especially for students who seem to naturally gravitate to that type of language.

EXAMPLE: Describe the Doppler effect with only rhyming nouns, no verbs.

Analogies

These can be drawings, words, or images that represent comparisons based on similarities.

Each of us has an outer and an inner mental life. The former uses ordinary language, but the latter cannot be expressed in words because of its complexity. So the goal is to use visual rather than verbal language to make these complex things, the human interactive things, visible, to give them form.

RAGE

HAPPINESS

SERENITY

HOPELESSNESS

Art can convey thought in such a way as to make it directly perceptible.

—Max Bill

EXAMPLE: Analogies can help students capture the essence of things; for example, "Draw an analogy for the core idea of the short story you just read."

The use of paradox: A statement exhibiting inexplicable or contradictory aspects, patterning balance and tensions in both verbal and nonverbal compositions.

Ask students, "What if the exact opposite is true? What would that be like?" Find ways to have your students illustrate the balance and the lack of balance that often exist together in compositions of all kinds—an invitation to take a deeper look. Examine the profound truth concerning balance in the universe. Use the behavior of subatomic systems to illustrate.

Three-Dimensional Tasks

Do building assignments, but not limited to only concrete tasks. Ask your students to create three-dimensional answers to the essential questions you pose in your major units. Have them build forms to illustrate their ideas and to show meanings.

EXAMPLE: Create a three-dimensional version of a core belief in a certain culture. This assignment would lead your students to examine the artifacts of that culture more closely.

Dramatics, Role Playing

Try all forms of role playing and creative dramatics. These engage the senses: visual, auditory, kinesthetic, etc. The creation of scripts involves interpersonal understandings. Have them write storylines that illustrate building tensions among individuals, and so on. This technique has so many positives, including great fun. Why teachers do not use it more is a real puzzle to me.

EXAMPLE: Create a role play wherein one of you is the father and one the son who just received a very poor report card. It is the first half of the son's senior year. (I actually did this one with a class of high school seniors, and the results were not only profound but also hilarious. Much good came out of that exchange.)

Clustering Disparate Things or Ideas Into New Groupings or Formations

This is the metaphor idea again. Putting multiple seemingly "dis-alike" things together in new ways is a challenge to the creative mode and a fine way to achieve new insights.

EXAMPLE: How is a corporation like a garden? Like a train station? Like plaster?

Movement, Kinesthetic Strategies

Ask your students to demonstrate understandings with body motion, especially without words. This reveals the underlying meanings of ideas. I remember a group of high school seniors who "performed" the process of photosynthesis in complete silence. Years later, ask them what they remember about that science class and they will say, "We remember photosynthesis."

Geometry

Geometry involves the measurements and relationships of points, lines, angles, surfaces, and solids. The spatial dimension of geometry puts it in a class by itself, so different from the left-mode processing of algebra. Notice the students who seem to take to geometry naturally. Some will tell you it is absolutely fascinating to them. There may be two entirely different ways to approach math: the logical–algebraic way and the visual–spatial way. Use the visual–spatial skills of geometry to examine illustrations of relationships in other content areas. Have your students demonstrate the essence of one of their essays visually. They can use circles within circles, arrows connecting parts, etc. An interesting fact is that in spite of the troubles in school experienced by Einstein, Edison, and da Vinci, they all shared a common trait: a natural interest and ability in geometry.

Most Math Conceptualizing

The mathematical thinker is one who, above all, is a student of puzzle forms. There are right- and left-mode aspects in the teaching of math. Set up discovery, bring forth the courage in your students to trust their own intuition, which precedes proof. Teach students to translate intuitive ideas into mathematical statements that can be tested.

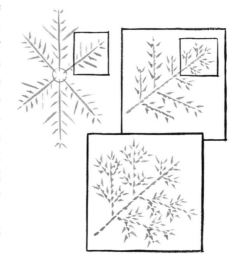

Math presents the most exciting possibilities for whole-brain strategies, and yet sadly most math is taught in only left-mode ways. "It is the intuitive mode that yields hypotheses quickly, interesting combinations of ideas before their worth is known. The intuitive insight is exactly what the techniques of analysis and proof are designed to test and check. It is founded on a kind of combinatorial playfulness . . . depending in great measure on the confidence one has in the process rather than on the right answers."[5]

Consider the math of music, of poetry, of great writing.

Finding Similarities Across Diverse Domains

If the teacher conceptualizes the issues well, the big ideas will present engaging combinations that students will discover across disciplines.

EXAMPLE: If the concept is "change," have students in your social studies class illustrate the concept from three different disciplines: science, human development theory, and their own community life.

Scanning is a vital skill that students need to master if they are to become adults who understand "the big picture" as well as the details. "Our left brains have become stiff with technique, far from the scanning eye."[6] Teach them to skim certain texts for the main idea, to scan a complicated work of art for just a few moments and then tell each other what they saw. Have them find patterns in the way their fellow students mingle, talk, and act on a minimally supervised playground.

Tinkering—All Kinds

Encourage your students to tinker. Give them permission to find things out for themselves. Set up experiments with many different possible and equally good results and conclusions. Their right brains will thank you.

Stream of Consciousness: Writing, Thinking, Journaling

Encourage this most subjective action as worthwhile and insightful. Let your students know that they know more than they know. Teach them to learn to trust their perceptions and emotions without worrying about whether something is said well or perfectly. The refinements come later; the insights are key here.

Using Color and Tone to Illustrate, to Compare, to Enrich

Use color to describe a person, a poem, a story, an idea.
EXAMPLE: If you had to choose a color to describe Huck Finn, what might it be? Would Tom Sawyer be a different color?

Parallel Processing

Try juxtaposing ideas (side by side) to better understand both.
EXAMPLE: Put the idea of chaos side by side with the idea of order. Can you find order in chaos and chaos in order? How? Give examples.

Body Language

All manner of body language skills engage the right mode. Your students will love this! Ask them in which situations they really need to understand body language and then have them simulate such situations for one another. The result is very insightful and goes much deeper into inter- and intrapersonal intelligence issues.

Reflective Dialogues in Which Language Is Used to Focus on the Mental States of Others

What was the main character feeling during this scene? If you were in that situation, what would you be feeling? Use this technique not only to understand literature but also to create original dramatic presentations.

Autobiographical Memories With Emotional Meaning

Have your students focus on memorable events in their lives, perhaps those that were turning points. The understandings from these insights may be used in a variety of ways: in original stories and dramatic presentations, juxtaposed beside a hero or heroine in a literature piece, or even examined through the lens of a musical piece. Students come to insightful understandings when they return to events that had great meaning. Ask a group of students to recount such events to one another, and have them create a short drama together illustrating a composite of these events. This is a very powerful process. Your students will learn much from one another.

Mindmapping in Action

These are stream-of-consciousness drawings in which one idea presents another and another. Ideas are drawn as they seem to relate to each other, using various shapes and directions. Used are both vertical operations, as in sets and subsets, as well as horizontal lines to indicate relationships.

Asking your students to create mindmaps is a brain- and memory-compatible strategy that greatly increases their understanding of the big picture. It also helps teachers have a sense of the important ideas that surround an idea. Use mindmaps to list all that is involved with a unit and as a double-check against standards (directly related and from other subject areas).

A student sample of "My Time"

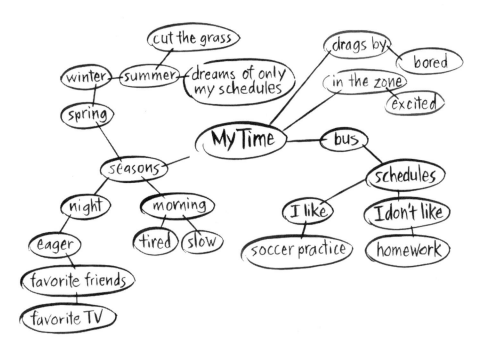

Try it! We have created some sample mindmaps. Fill in some of the blanks, then add your own branches. Try creating interactive mindmaps on the board. Try creating mindmaps that "grow" over the course of a unit. If you have access to the Inspiration software, use it in front of the classroom for brainstorming sessions.

1. Unit-based

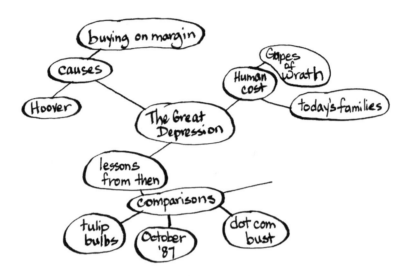

2. Curriculum-based

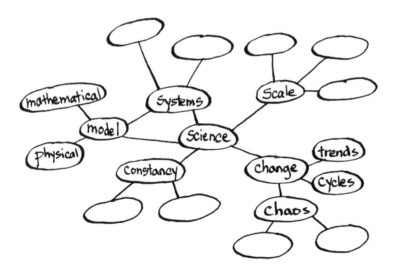

Try sharing *all* the connections with students. You'll be surprised at how much of the big picture they can see. We've left some balloons empty for you to fill in on your own. Feel free to add spokes.

3. Concept-based

After you have brainstormed some of the ideas for this concept-based mindmap, consider it against your standards requirements. Can you relate particular standards to these ideas?

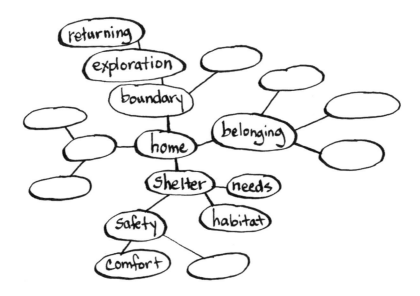

Nonverbal Representations of All Types

Use symbols, shapes, literal representations, and nonliteral representations (squiggles, vortex-type delineations, etc.) to illustrate understanding.

EXAMPLE: Use a nonverbal series of only lines (no literal pictures) to capture what you think is the essence of the short story *A Separate Piece.*

Examples

Science

Students create a bird of their own design using torn-up paper. What features are important?

Students create a visual or three-dimensional metaphor of refraction.

Math

Students record and draw patterns found in nature.

In groups, students demonstrate imbalance kinesthetically, artistically, and dramatically.

Social Studies

Students draw a picture of what the world would look like if there were no rules.

Students create a media collage depicting gender stereotypes.

Language

Students create a visual analog portraying the feeling of being walled out or walled in.

Students create an interpretive symbol of a poem, then capture the essence with a word or short phrase.

Now you try. Brainstorm nonverbal representation examples for:

growth	functions	impact of technology
cells	sets	haiku
equilibrium	estimation	sentence structure
interconnectedness of living things	scarcity	short story
adaptation	political systems	persuasion
place value	supply and demand	public speaking
fractions	trade among nations	created with Inspiration

Brainstorm other ideas with peers and be sure to include art and music.

Now try it with things you are teaching.

Use this mini-worksheet to brainstorm your ideas for using nonverbal representation in the classroom. While there is no specific formula for these ideas, they all share common elements. They are nonreading and nonwriting expressions of ideas and understandings.

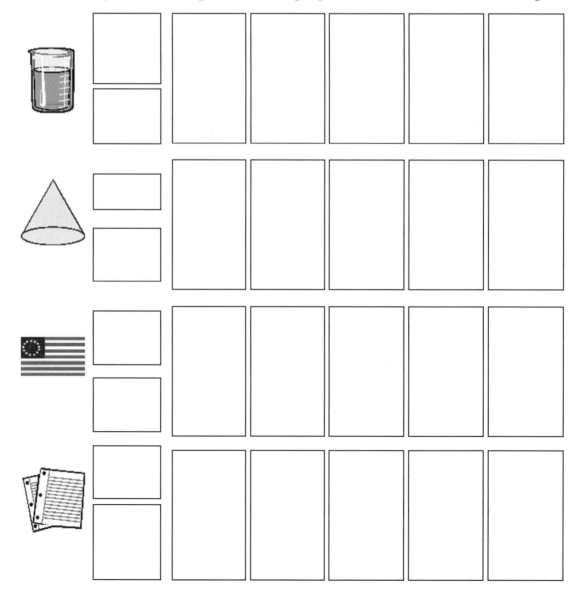

Using Music to Accompany, Compare, Augment, or Even Explain

Music is seldom used well, even by music teachers. Think of explaining a short story with a musical composition that illustrates the same mood, issues, or emotion. The word music comes from a Latin root meaning "art of the muses."

> *It is generally agreed that Mozart used G minor to express melancholy. The Greeks linked certain musical modes to particular emotions.*
>
> —Anthony Storr

There is music in so many things: feelings, nuance, self-expression, the way we converse. Music can be used to convey meaning in a way that nothing else can. It is texture in the air.

Music is proof of the inexpressible. For those who don't yet possess the gifts of the poet, music can convey feelings that are impossible to articulate with words.

EXAMPLE: Ask students to liken punctuation to musical rests, symbols, dynamics, and directions, writing the same "sentence" with words, then with music, then perhaps with movement.

Have your students take a main emotion from a piece of literature and match it to a piece of music.

> *Musical training is a more potent instrument than any other, because rhythm and harmony find their way into the inward places of the soul, resulting in gracefulness.*
>
> —Anthony Storr

EXAMPLE: Use music to set tones in your classrooms. What kind of music would you use to introduce binomials in algebra or James Joyce's *The Dubliners* in Senior Lit? How can you incorporate popular music (the music your students listen to) into your classroom?

Use this mini-worksheet to brainstorm the possible uses of music in the regular classroom. Don't forget to invite a music teacher or musician!

Examples in Social Studies and Literature

What music was important at this time in history?

Is there any particular style of music that defined this era?

Are there parallels between the characteristics of the music of the time and the characteristics of the visual art or literature? For example, Impressionistic music and Impressionistic art share softness, lack of linearity, etc.

Your examples

Examples in Science and Math

Is there music that characterizes this concept?

Try Stravinsky for chaos; try a Bach fugue for balance.

Your examples

Examples in any subject

Can music be used to introduce a new idea dramatically?

Is there a musical metaphor for this thing? For example, punctuation with musical notation, rhythm with mathematical patterns, the movement of light with the movement of sound, musical expression and dynamics with literary expression.

Your examples

Demonstrations

The act of presenting information in ways that have to be used, rather than just explained, calls upon a plethora of expertise. Successful demonstrations require students to produce a number of things. They need good visuals or working models. They need to interact with their audience and possess a real grasp of the material they are presenting. Create specific rubrics (lists of criteria) for exemplary demonstrations.

There are multiple advantages to demonstrations.

They allow you to delve deeper into a subject (a must in the current climate of "coverage first").

They allow you to create individual or group "student experts."

They force students to get to know the content at a deeper level.

They allow for different representations of understanding, capitalizing on learner diversity.

This well-rounded approach to assessment raises the odds that learners will "get it" and retain it.

Technology plays an important role in these demonstrations. Many schools have demonstration tools that rival what is available in corporate boardrooms. You can use these tools to allow learners to express understanding in multiple ways.

Try the mini-worksheet that follows to help you start thinking about creative demonstrations in the classroom. Be sure to think in terms of authoring tools and multiple media.

Example in Language

Create a slideshow that combines still images, music, and dramatic reading to portray the feeling of a poet's work.

Your examples for sentence structure: for _____. (your content choice)

Example in Science

Create a PowerPoint presentation that compares and contrasts how different forms and structures reflect different functions (e.g., similarities and differences among animals that fly, walk, or swim). Present and narrate.

Your examples for photosynthesis: for _____. (your content choice)

Example in Social Studies

Create a Web site that examines two differing perspectives on the separation of church and state with links to articles, images, and guided presentation.

Your examples for ancient people: for _____. (your content choice)

Example in Math

Use iMovie to present a top 10 list of algebra in the world.

Your examples for set operations: for _____. (your content choice)

HUNCHING

Encourage your students to follow a hunch. Set up situations in which hunching is valued, and help them analyze the steps they follow in order to confirm or rule out their hunches. Try an experiment in science, or an idea about why someone acted the way they did, followed by an interview to confirm or rule out or a search for the root cause of a complicated problem.

This is problem–solution-based teaching. It taps directly into the creative imaginations of learners and intrigues them when solutions "become informed." It also allows teachers to steer learners in a sudden new direction, examining different perspectives.

Try the sample worksheet to start adding hunching to your classroom.

Examples in Literature

The Problem: Bigotry and Uninformed Perceptions

Supporting Content: *To Kill a Mockingbird*

Hunch This: What changes could be made in this school so that everyone were treated as they should be treated?

The Problem: Scarcity

Supporting Content: *Grapes of Wrath*

Hunch This: What would you do if you had to suddenly raise your family on one-tenth of your present income?

Your example

The Problem:

Supporting Content:

Hunch This:

Example in Social Studies

The Problem: Social Chaos

Supporting Content: Rules in society

Hunch This: What would this school look like if there were no rules? Would even the students want just a few rules? Which rules would they add first?

Your example

The Problem:

Supporting Content:

Hunch This:

Example in English/Language Arts

The Problem: Communicating emotion in written form

Supporting Content: Poetry

Hunch This: What process do you suppose poets go through as they attempt to "find the right words" to portray deep feelings and emotions?

Your example

The Problem:

Supporting Content:

Hunch This:

Examples in Math

The Problem: Unknowns

Supporting Content: Variables

Hunch This: How might you gauge the opinions of 1000 people on 20 different questions? Would you use a computer? What would the computer have to do?

The Problem: Hitting a Target

Supporting Content: Cartesian Coordinate System

Hunch This: Try hitting a target with a makeshift cannon. How might you succeed 100% of the time? Can you develop a system that makes it possible for anyone to hit the target using any cannon?

Your example

The Problem:

Supporting Content:

Hunch This:

Example in Science

The Problem: Your species is becoming extinct

Supporting Content: Adaptation

Hunch This: What do you hunch needs to be present in the environment for a species to survive? Why do you suppose some species are able to succeed in the seemingly hostile environment of encroaching development while others die?

Your example

The Problem:

Supporting Content:

Hunch This:

Graphic Organizers

Graphic organizers have been around for some time, but it is only when the right-mode research began to surface that educators realized their power for increasing understanding. The use of a visual representation of a concept, an idea, an event, or a story line illustrates not only the idea but also the spatial relationships and hence the connections between the parts.

Try using graphic organizers with all your content, and even make them part of your assessments. Practice with these and pay particular attention to the process you go through in creating them.

Create a graphic image of cause and effect.

Create a graphic to show the story line in *Little Red Riding Hood*.

Create a graphic organizer to show a sequence of events.

Share these with your peers.

Now try the following:

Use an image technique to teach the concept of community caring.

Use a metaphor to teach how we draw conclusions.

Use round thinking to examine the strategies used in a historical battle.

Use patterning to teach the early explorers of this continent.

Use a graphic organizer to teach a story line.

Now take one of your own lessons, add a graphic organizer technique, and teach the lesson with it added. Note what happens to your students. Share what happens with a peer, coach, or group.

How vital are graphic organizers to help students understand? Help each other come up with more ways to use roundness.

Your activity before graphic organizer enhancement:

Your activity after graphic organizer enhancement:

What happened when you tried it?

Howard Gardner (1999) afforded special status to images, metaphors, patterns, and graphic organizers.

Thomas West, speaking of Gardner's thinking on this status:

"The special status Gardner accords this mode of thought is underlined by his concluding observations about it. Gardner indicates that there is evidence that this particular mode has greater longevity in individuals, and may be associated in a fundamental way with what we know as wisdom. Here, once again, is the preoccupation with wholes rather than parts, with patterns rather than pieces, with similarities rather than differences."

In Gardner's own words:

"My own view is that each form of intelligence has a natural life course: while logical–mathematical thought proves fragile later in life, across all individuals . . . certain aspects of visual and spatial knowledge prove robust, especially in individuals who have practiced them regularly throughout their lives. There is a sense of the whole which seems to be a reward for aging—a continuing perhaps even an enhanced capacity to appreciate the whole, to discern patterns even when certain details or fine points may be lost. Perhaps wisdom draws on this."

Finish this sentence and share your conclusion with your peers:

A life of schooling with no attention to the whole brain and the cycle would lead to . . .

NOTES

1. West 1991.
2. Frost 1951.
3. Gleick 1987.
4. Benson and Zaidel 1985.
5. Bruner 1966, 1979.
6. Ibid.

5

Overlaying Right- and Left-Mode to Complete the 4MAT Cycle

The last step in understanding the complete 4MAT cycle is the overlay of right- and left-mode processing strategies in each of the four quadrants. The purpose of Quadrant One is to create meaning, to answer the question "Why?" The right mode is sensory; it comes from feeling. It synthesizes, puts things together. Begin with the right mode.

STEP 1: CONNECT

Establish a relationship between your learners and the content, connecting it to their lives—not telling them how it connects, but having something actually happen in the classroom that will help them make the connection themselves. The experience you create must be based on the essence of the content.

connect

STEP 2: ATTEND

Have your students analyze what just happened. Have them attend to their own experience and to the perceptions of their fellow students—how it went, what really happened.

attend

Allow students to reflect on the experience together, discussing, sharing, seeing similar patterns. After the created experience, have your students examine what just happened; have them step outside the experience, applying the left mode's analyzing skill—standing aside to better understand. If you have established a climate of trust (so necessary for all real learning), your students will become mentors to each other.

As they step outside the experience to discuss it, they will help each other understand the value of the material, the relationships, the discrepancies, and the inherent possibilities.

The Quadrant One processing steps are connect and attend:

Connect: *co nectere*—to bind with

Attend: *ad tendere*—to stretch toward

The purpose of Quadrant Two is to inform and enlarge the learner's understanding of the content, to answer the question "What?" Bring the right mode to bear on the concept under study before you deliver the expert knowledge.

image

STEP 3: IMAGINE

You need your students to imagine, to picture the concept as they understand it and have experienced it, before you take them to the experts (for example, Einstein seeing light curving).

Right-mode activities such as analogies, metaphors, and visuals that capture the conceptual essence (as it is currently known by your students) will bring them to the expert content, not as "strangers in a strange land" but as persons who can say "I already know something about this."

inform

STEP 4: INFORM

Students are now ready for the left-mode step of Quadrant Two, receiving and examining the expert knowledge. Inform them of the content they need to understand; give them the expert knowledge.

This is the telling time, a receiving time for your students. This is where a fine, organized, well-delivered lecture belongs—illuminating texts, guest speakers, films, information from Web sources, CDs, etc.

If you do this well, you prepare your students to take the learning away from you and the experts and to begin to take ownership of it for themselves.

The Quadrant Two processing steps are imagine and inform:

Imagine: *imaginen*—to create a mental picture

Inform: *in forma*—to bring form into

The purpose of Quadrant Three is to practice, to become skilled, to move to mastery, to answer the question "How?"

STEP 5: PRACTICE

practice

Stay first with the left mode. Your students must practice the learning as the experts do it. It is not yet time for innovation or adaptation.

They need to learn by practicing. They need to become sufficiently skilled before they can innovate. Think of a musician: practice first, then interpret. Create work practice that is fun yet demanding.

Facilitate moving through the activities, the centers you create to help them achieve mastery. When a sufficient level of skill has been reached, your students can begin to extend the learning into their lives.

STEP 6: EXTEND

extend

This is where innovation begins. Students know enough; they have enough skills to tinker, to see how it works for them, to play with the content, the skills, the materials, the ideas, the wholes and the parts, the details, the data and the big picture. They can make something of this learning for themselves, be interpretive.

The right mode's ability to see possibilities, patterns, wholeness, and roundness is a major asset here. There is no set path, just the processing. Now the various centers in the classroom become very busy. There is no set-in-stone algorithm, just hunches and nuances. There is no sequence; insights arrive as the doing comes together. When this happens in a classroom, it is really something to see.

This is when students and teacher engage in major quality time! Every time I witness it, I am uplifted.

The Quadrant Three processing steps are practice and extend:

Practice: *praktikos*—capable of being used

Extend: *ex tendere*—to stretch out of

(Note the step in the cycle opposite this, Attend, to stretch toward. The notion of opposites moves through the entire cycle, a key invitation to growth.)

Note the step opposite this on the wheel, Attend (to stretch toward) leads to Extend (to stretch outward) in this step, as the learning becomes active. The notion of opposites moves through the entire cycle, a key invitation to growth.

The purpose of Quadrant Four is to adapt, to create, to integrate the learning so it can be used by the students in their future, to answer the question "If?"

refine

STEP 7: REFINE

Again stay with the left mode. The students have proposed an extension of the learning into their lives. They need to evaluate that extension in the cool light of left-mode analysis. Remember that the left mode is a stepping back. Other students can critique (students are often the best evaluators of their own work). The teacher suggests, helps with resources, offers. Have them move outside of their own extension, analyzing, improving, refining their work.

perform

STEP 8: PERFORM

Last, have your students perform. Look for originality, relevance, new questions, connections to larger ideas, skills that are immediately useful, values confirmed or questioned anew.

Here the students display their understanding, how relevant the content is to them, its connection to larger ideas, how it fits into their world. Values are confirmed or challenged; knowledge assumes new form. The students are now the true center of the action; the context of the student now embodies the text of the experts.

The Quadrant Four processing steps are refine and perform:

Refine: *re fin*—back again, to limit, to end, to explore the boundary or limit again

Perform: *per form*—to form through, to shape, to mold, to fashion

Note the step opposite this on the wheel, Inform (to add form into) leads to Perform (to form *through*) in this culminating step. The notion of opposites moves through the entire cycle, a key invitation to growth.

All Real Learning Leaves Us Changed

6

Teaching From Concepts

Teaching with 4MAT requires that teachers create a feeling-level experience at the outset of each lesson, a connection to the learner. This connection requires that teachers teach from rich concepts. For example, a 4MAT teacher setting out to deliver material on Christopher Columbus would have difficulty creating a connection to learner meaning. The answer to the question "How do learners have an existing meaning connection to Christopher Columbus?" might be, "They don't!" To create that connection, teachers must think big. We ask teachers to "umbrella" their content, to identify the big idea that overarches content. In our Christopher Columbus example, the big idea might be something like "exploration." Now consider the possibilities of connecting learners to exploration—breaking boundaries, why do people feel the need to explore, to move beyond, how is the concept of home related to the concept of exploring—the possibilities abound. This is a much easier exercise than connecting them to Christopher Columbus.

WHAT WAS THAT ABOUT?

Imagine you have just left a movie with friends, and someone asks, "What was that movie really about?" And before you can answer, one member of your party says, "Betrayal; the movie was about betrayal!"

You realize that this answer has cut through all the details—the sequence of events, the atmosphere the director has set so painstakingly, the cast of characters—and named precisely the core theme of the film. You are struck by the keenness of mind it takes to do that and by the artistry of the filmmaker who pulled it off.

Or consider teaching *Macbeth* to your students. Perhaps betrayal is the core concept. You could design a lesson that would weave betrayal throughout, pulling from students' personal experiences. If you are asked to consider the color red, your brain would be able to look around and see all the examples and patterns of red—in an instant. In a similar sense, you can ask learners to examine all the instances of betrayal in the play and in their lives. They will begin to see it all around them. With this simple emphasis you will have created recognition, retention, and meaning.

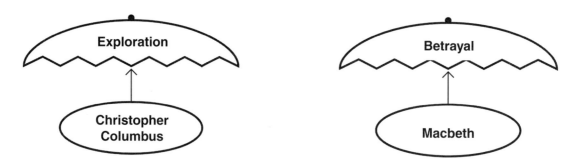

WORKING WITH CONCEPTS

A concept is a significant idea that relates to other significant ideas in a way that connects to the main body of content and creates meaning for students in their lives. A topic is a subset of a concept, a smaller section of content that specifies the particulars.

How do you decide which is which? How does an idea get "concept status"? There are no hard and fast rules. The answer is, it depends.

It depends on the context, the learners, the time and place. It depends on teachers and how well they know their students. An idea is a concept when it naturally connects: to learners, to content, and to other significant ideas. A good concept will present cross-discipline possibilities, e.g., exploration in Science, Social Studies, Literature, Music, etc. The following pages will help you understand the difference between concepts and topics and how this applies to your teaching.

DIFFERENT TEACHERS, DIFFERENT CONCEPTS

It is important to note that different teachers will define concepts differently, with equally good results. In a lesson covering Romantic poets, one teacher realized that these poets were very often rebels of their times, and their poetry was an expression of the need to assert their individuality. She shaped the lesson around the concept of individuality and the need to be self-expressive. Another teacher saw the common thread among the same poets as their awe of natural beauty. She chose the concept of beauty and the ways people express their appreciation of beauty and shaped the lesson around that concept.

Two teachers with the exact same content used different concepts, both with great results in terms of learner engagement, resonance, retention, and creative adaptation of material learned. When creating concepts, trust your own insights as to what might resonate most with your students.

See if you can distinguish between a concept and a topic. Which items would you consider concepts and which would you consider topics?

structure (as in Science)

tides

root words

quality

human systems (as in Social Studies)

percentage

magnets

the Dark Ages

the Civil War

force

List five concepts in any discipline that you believe should be taught to all students.

1.

2.

3.

4.

5.

Share these with your peer group.

One way teachers can recognize the difference between concepts and topics is by asking, "What is this a study in?" For example, you could say that Christopher Columbus is a study in exploration. Keeping this in mind, consider the next list, categorized by subject areas. Play with these areas as concepts and also as topics. If you decide to make them topical, then name the concept they might serve.

Social Studies

Continuity in Human Culture   Fossil Fuels

The American Family   Interdependence of Peoples

Basic Human Needs   First Amendment Rights

Grain: Basic Food for Humanity   Environmental Influences

Arms Negotiations   The Migrations of People

Science

Plants   Stars

Energy   Air Pollution

Diastrophism (Movement of   Volcanoes
the Earth's Crust)

Solar System   The Scientist

UFOs   Genetic Manipulation

Math

Decimals   Zero

Functions   Line

Value   Ratio

Binary Systems   Place Value

Volume   Exponents

Plane

Literature

The Novel	Myth
Drama as Social Criticism	Fiction
Realism	Literary Methods
Characterization	Impressionism
The Short Story	Reading
The Humorists	Syntax

Parts of Speech

Vowels	Sequencing
Comprehension	Consonant Blends
Main Ideas	Pattern Recognition
Context	Inferences

Music

Rhythm	Counterpoint
Meter	Fugue
Criticism	12-Bar Blues
Tempo	Sonata Form
Jazz	Timbre
Impressionism	Form
Rubato	Modality

Visual Arts

Composition	Negative Space
Expression	Perspective
Impressionism	

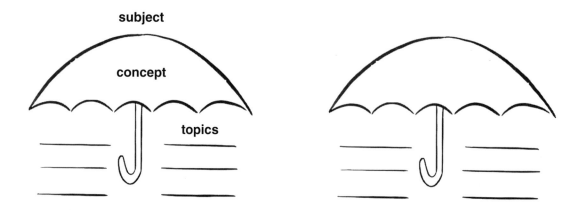

CONCEPTS AND STANDARDS

Look at the following standards.[1] See if there are concepts embedded in them that might help students establish personal connections. Choose one and work through the best conceptual approach you can envision.

Language Arts—Writing

Uses strategies to organize written work (e.g., includes a beginning, middle, and ending; uses a sequence of events).

Language Arts—Speech

Uses content, style, and structure that is appropriate for specific audiences; that is, formal or informal language, public or private communications, with the different purposes of entertaining, influencing, or informing.

Math

Understands that some events are more likely to happen than others.
Understands that the word "chance" refers to the likelihood of an event.

Science

Knows that plants and animals progress through life cycles of birth, growth and development, reproduction, and death; the details of these life cycles are different for different organisms.
Knows that the strength of the electric force between two charged objects is proportional to the charges (opposite charges attract, whereas like charges repel) and, as with gravitation, is inversely proportional to the square of the distance between them.

UMBRELLA AS A VERB

The process we use for conceptualizing content is called The Umbrella Exercise. You write the description of the content you hope to teach in the oval at the bottom of the page, as illustrated below, and then attempt to find the overarching idea and write it into the umbrella that covers the oval. The umbrella/oval is a graphic organizer that helps clarify the best way to approach the content. The concept you choose to write in your umbrella is the idea that is implicit in the content and connects best to your students.

When you "umbrella" a topic, you find its essence. For example, photosynthesis might umbrella up to growth, equations in algebra to balance. A lesson on the holocaust might umbrella to dehumanization. 4MAT lessons begin with this content essence. These umbrellas can be thought of as overarching not only the content but every element of the unit. These concepts guide lesson authors and students through each step of the 4MAT process.

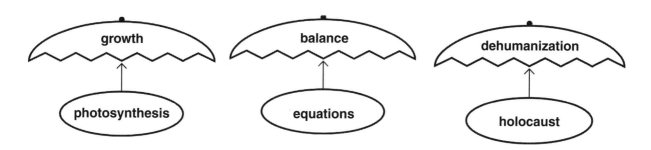

EXPLORATION AS AN EXAMPLE

We chose exploration as an umbrella concept for Christopher Columbus. Think of the idea of exploration. All humans have a need to break boundaries, to reach higher. All humans are intrigued by the unknown. Is the need to explore part of our makeup? What of the equally important human needs to settle down, to build something lasting? How are these dichotomous ideas related?

Exploration is a significant idea that relates to other significant ideas in a way that connects to the main body of the Social Studies content and has great potential for creating meaning in students' lives. While there are no hard and fast rules for determining concepts, there are some guidelines.

MORE PRACTICE WITH UMBRELLA CONCEPTS

The ideas below are significant enough to qualify as concepts. Does each fulfill our definition of a concept? We have filled in some sample concepts from various subject areas. Now add your ideas, based on your understanding of these subjects and your familiarity with your curriculum and standards.

Literature

Our concept is: Heroism

Our concept is: The Novel

Other significant concepts might be:

1. _____

2. _____

3. _____

Grammar

Our concept is: The Sentence

Other significant concepts might be:

1. _____

2. _____

3. _____

Writing

Our concept is: Expression

Other significant concepts might be:

1. _____

2. _____

3. _____

Music

Our concept is: Rhythm. There are great possibilities here—cycles of life, both biological and emotional, tides (using ocean sounds, day and night, seasons, etc.).

Other significant concepts might be:

1. _____

2. _____

3. _____

Math

Our concept is: Balance

Other significant concepts might be:

1. _____

2. _____

3. _____

Science

Our concept is: Living and Nonliving Things

Other significant concepts might be:

1. _____

2. _____

3. _____

You are encouraged to challenge our choice of concepts. We stress the need for teachers to build their own conceptual structures to relate and organize content and standards for them. These decisions must be made in the context of their learners.

While there are significant ideas in any content area that are basic to understanding that content, there are also many choices that can be made, choices that will form meaningful connections for particular students in particular places in particular times. Even in the current climate of micromanagement of curriculum, these choices must be left to master teachers.

4MAT IN ACTION!

What Are the Concepts That Overarch the Things You Teach?

Now look at lessons you are currently teaching or developing. Think about them in terms of 4MAT. The following sections will build on each other. So work completed in this section, for example, carries over to the next section. Have your lessons in front of you as you perform these exercises.

For each of the units you are working on, complete the Concept-Finding Worksheet that follows.

Concept-Finding Worksheet

"What's important here?"

1. What is the lesson's title?

2. What is the lesson about?

3. Does the above definition capture the very essence of the lesson? If not, think about what ideas might overarch your response above and experiment with those ideas using the following queries.

4. Is that a significant idea?

5. Does it relate to other significant ideas in a way that connects to the main body of the content?

6. Does it have potential for creating meaning in students' lives?

7. What is it a study in? The harder this is, the bigger your ideas may be. If, for example, you decide that exploration is a study in exploration, you're on the right track.

8. In what ways do your students encounter this regularly? Are their lives or the lives of their family and friends touched by it?

9. What would happen if it didn't exist? Would that be a problem?

10. Does it relate to other ideas in other subjects? All the most important ideas touch every corner of every subject (and human endeavor). A good concept will have numerous associations to other areas of life and study.

11. How would your students be personally affected by an internalization of this concept—not just knowing about it, but having it be a part of them?

12. How would it look in the center of a mindmap? A good concept makes a good hub for a mindmap. Try it! Sketch a quick associative map of your main idea in the space below. Doodle your concept mindmap here. Feel free to add balloons.

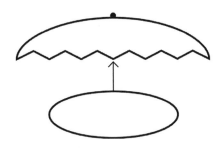

Most important, if you feel that your unit essence is not quite big enough, don't sweat it. Come up with some other ideas that you feel do overarch your unit. If you're wrong, you'll discover later that the main concept choice may need tweaking, as you try to connect to learners in Quadrant One, for example. Umbrella your concept here.

NOTE

1. From the Mid-continent Research for Education and Learning (McREL) list.

The 4MAT Design Overlay (Lesson Planning)

How do teachers look at what they are already doing through the lens of the 4MAT framework? The instructions that follow will help teachers create a 4MAT Wheel by reflecting on or adapting what they are already doing.

THE INFORMATION DELIVERY

What will be your information delivery system? You should avoid using only text and lecture for information delivery. How will you tell students about the content? Are you going to lecture? Will the lecture be interactive (stopping along the way and interacting with students or asking them to do something)? Is there possibly a guest lecturer? Will there be assigned readings? Could technology or media be used to enrich your information delivery? Fill in your information delivery process description in Quadrant Two, Left Mode on the 4MAT Wheel.

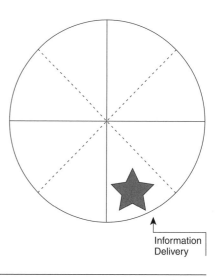

Information Delivery

THE SKILLS PRACTICE

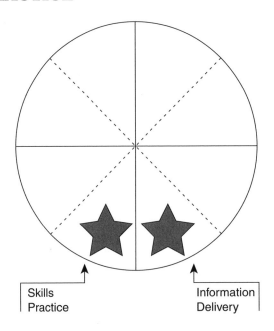

Skills
Practice

Information
Delivery

How will you determine if they understood the lecture?

What kind of practice will you require?

Are there work pages or questions at the end of chapters?

Are there skill and drill materials?

Fill in your process description in Quadrant Three, Left Mode.

THE INTENDED OUTCOMES

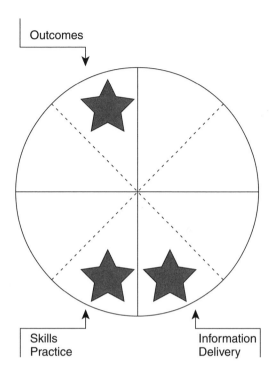

What outcomes are you intending for students?

What will they be able to do that they can't do now?

How will they synthesize their learning?

Will they share reading notes, graphic organizers, summaries of important events, their personal reflections, their visuals?

Will you have them create a composite representation of their "learnings"?

The word "per-form" means "to form through." Ultimately, this step represents the merging of the learning and the learner. How will learners explain or perform their work? Avoid a series of reports during which they stand up and deliver while fellow students endure. This is not learning. Student reports, one after another, can be more deadly than a boring teacher.

Fill in the expected outcome in Quadrant Four, Right Mode.

THE CONNECTION

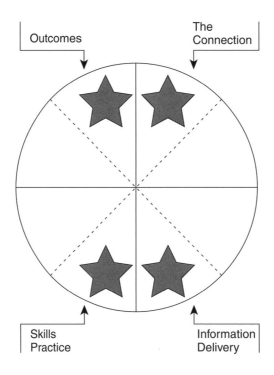

What will you do to get your students excited about the material?

What experience will you create in the classroom that will lead them to want to know what you're about to teach?

Remember, this is never telling; this is something that happens, something that intrigues them (a problem to solve), connects to them (a situation that has real meaning in their lives), or touches them in a way that links to their humanity.

Fill in that connection experience in Quadrant One, Right Mode.

SHARING THE CONNECTION

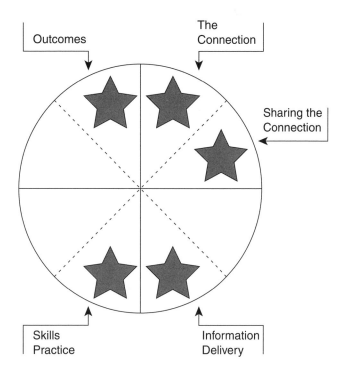

What discussion techniques will you use to give students the opportunity to share what just happened in the experience you created?

How will you have them discuss their perceptions? Will it be teacher-directed (the least potent), a small group discussion with cooperative learning techniques, or student partners?

Will you ask them to list any commonalities they have discovered in their shared perceptions? Will these lists be shared with the entire group?

Will you ask them to write reflections, perhaps in journals, on the connections they experienced through the discussion?

Will you ask them to list "hoped-for" outcomes of the learning they are about to experience?

List the process you will use to amplify the connections in Quadrant One, Left Mode.

THE LEARNING USED

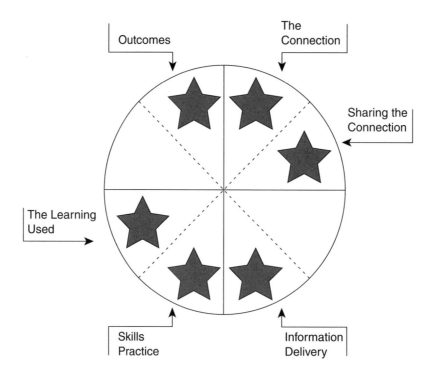

This is where students take learning and do something with it, something that has meaning for them, not just something that is done to pass a test for school's sake. This is where relevance is demonstrated.

Where does your concept exist in life outside school? Where is it useful?

Can you ask learners to answer these questions and find these applications?

Can you give learners an opportunity to interpret material, to adapt it to their lives and unique perspectives?

What will they do to show and use their new understandings and new skills? Choose projects or performance requirements that are meaningful and useful in the students' own lives.

Fill in the description of what you will ask of them in Quadrant Three, Right Mode.

CRITIQUING THE WORK

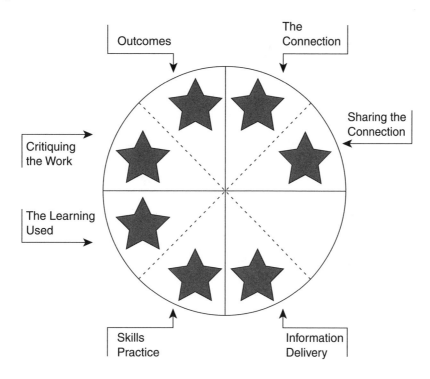

How will students edit and refine their unique use of the learning? Here they pause to reflect, merging their interpretive applications with "by the book."

What procedures will you put in place for feedback and mentoring?

Will you use peer review? Self-evaluation?

Could student self-evaluations be linked back to the Quadrant One, Left Mode step, where "hoped-for" outcomes were written as part of their reflections?

Fill in the critiquing and refinement procedures you will use in Quadrant Four, Left Mode.

THE IMAGE THAT CONNECTS

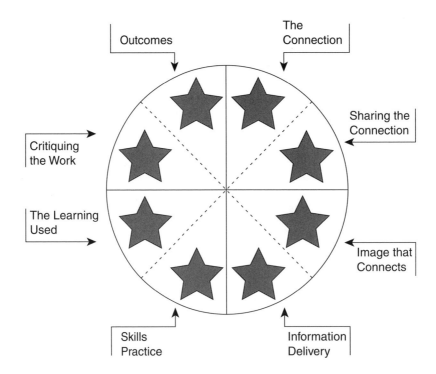

What is the nonverbal strategy you will use to have learners express their "pre-understanding" of the concept? For example, if you are studying rebellion, have them draw a need to rebel. If you are studying decay, have them nonverbally express a lack of decay. If you are studying liberty, have them recite poems and play songs that express freedom. These expressions must be based directly on the learners' past experiences, as connected and shared in Quadrant One, and must relate to the content you are explaining in the lecture/readings that follow. If you do this well, the students will attend to your lecture and focus on their readings with a highly successful attitude of "Oh! I know what this means; I have experienced this."

A note about image strategies: We use the word "nonverbal" to move teachers away from the often tedious overkill of text. However, a fine piece of poetry can capture images with great power.

ADDING THE ASSESSMENTS

The heart of assessment is really: How are my students doing?

Even though we must know—"did they do it?" we must also keep track of their progress along the way so we can monitor and adjust. That is how we ensure they are able to do it.

As students travel the cycle, you should check on their progress at five key places.

1. At the End of Quadrant One

   Did the groups/partners work well together?

   Did the experience you created enable them to make a personal connection?

   Were their perceptions shared honestly and enriched by this sharing?

   How will you know?

2. Can students depict the meaning of the Quadrant One experience as a concept, a significant idea that the details in the lecture will exemplify?

   Did the graphic organizer/visual representation, poetic/musical strategy help them to see the big picture, the core meaning of the content?

   How will you know?

3. After the Information Delivery

   Did they understand the material?

   Do they know the difference between the important information versus the substantiating details?

   What kind of test, quiz, or oral exchange will help you find out?

4. After the Skills Practice
   Can they do it?

   Can they do it as you taught it? This is important because students need the expert skill base practiced and fluid before they can move on to adapting the learning to new or novel situations.

   What kind of measurements will you use to ascertain their skill level?

5. At the End of the Performance/Project/Personal Extension
   What outcome are you after?

   How will you know they accomplished it?

   What rubric will you use, what list of criteria for different grades, for an A or a B, etc.?

   Will you involve students in creating the rubric?

   Will you ask them to provide new questions as part of their ending?

   Will you ask them what they learned that you didn't ask?

   How will you combine the various assessment parts into one final grade?

YOUR 4MAT PLAN: A FINAL LOOK

Use these eight questions as a final check of your 4MAT plan.

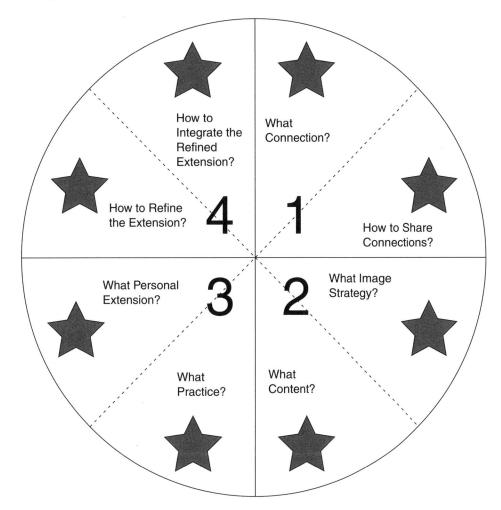

Epilogue

IN ALL OF THIS, REMEMBER THE CHILDREN

When a student is bored,

has no heart for learning,

no motivation to grow,

the great gift of inner light is imprisoned,

the light that beholds itself

is hesitant and dim.

We must open a way for that uniqueness,

that glow, to create new clearings,

new possibilities for transformation.

We need to commit our students to meaning.

That is the great task of teaching.

The future of the children,

all the children,

is what we owe to life.

The teacher who moves us to growth,

is the greatest of gifts,

one to be prized above all others.

If, in every classroom,

we had a master teacher,

the world would be transformed.

Bibliography

Abraham, R. H., & Shaw, C. D. (1984). *Dynamics—the geometry of behavior, part I: Periodic behavior.* Santa Cruz, CA: Aerial.

Aitken, K. J., & Trevarthen, C. (1997). Self-other organization in human psychological development. *Development and Psychopathology, 9,* 653–677.

Baker, E. L., Freeman, M., & Clayton, S. (1990). *Cognitive assessment of subject matter: Understanding the marriage of psychological theory and educational policy in achievement testing* (CSE Technical Rep. No. 317). Los Angeles: UCLA Center for Research on Evaluation, Standards, and Student Testing.

Benson, D. F. (1994). *The neurology of thinking.* New York: Oxford University Press.

Benson, D. F., & Zaidel, E. (Eds.). (1985). *The dual brain: Hemispheric specialization in humans.* New York: Guilford Press.

Bogen, J. (1986). Mental duality in the intact brain. *Bulletin of Clinical Neurosciences, 51,* 3–29.

Bohm, D. (1996). *Wholeness and the implicate order.* London: Routledge.

Bradshaw, J., & Nettleton, N. (1983). *Human cerebral asymmetry.* Englewood Cliffs, NJ: Prentice Hall.

Bransford, J. (1999). *How people learn: Brain, mind, experience, and school.* Washington, DC: National Academy Press.

Bruner, J. (1966). *Toward a theory of instruction.* Cambridge, MA: Harvard University Press.

Bruner, J. (1979). *On knowing: Essays for the left hand.* Cambridge, MA: Harvard University Press.

Carroll, L. (1995). *The complete illustrated works.* New York: Random House.

Cook-Greuter, S. R. (1995). *Comprehensive language awareness: A definition of the phenomenon and a review of its treatment in the post-formal adult development literature.* Unpublished doctoral dissertation, Harvard University Graduate School of Education.

Damasio, A. (1999). *The feeling of what happens: Body and emotion in the making of consciousness.* New York: Harcourt Brace.

Defanti, T., Brown, M., & McCormick, B. (1989). Visualization: Expanding scientific and engineering research opportunities. *Computer, 22,* 12–25.

Dewey, J. (1934). *Art as experience.* New York: Perigee Books.

Dewey, J. (1938). *Experience and education.* New York: Macmillan.

Dewey, J. (1986). How we think: A restatement of the relation of reflective thinking to the educative process. In J. A. Boydston (Ed.), *John Dewey: The later works, 1925–1953.* Carbondale: Southern Illinois University Press.

Diamond, M. C. (1988). *Enriching heredity: The impact of the environment on the anatomy of the brain.* New York: The Free Press.

Dillard, A. (1974). *Pilgrim at Tinker Creek.* Cutchogue, NY: Buccaneer Books.

Dreyfus, S., & Dreyfus, H. (1985). *Mind over machine: The power of human intuition and expertise in the era of the computer.* New York: Macmillan.

Elliott Eisner, personal communication, 2004.

Freire, P. (1970). *Pedagogy of the oppressed.* New York: Continuum.

Frost, R. (1951). The figure a poem makes. In *Complete poems* (E. C. Lathem, ed.). London: Jonathan Cape. R*evolution.* New York: Basic Books.

Gardner, H. (1993). *Frames of mind: The theory of multiple intelligences.* New York: Basic Books.

Gardner, H. (1999). *Intelligence reframed.* New York: Basic Books.

Gazzaniga, M. S. (1992). *Nature's mind: The biological roots of thinking, emotions, sexuality, language, and intelligence.* New York: Basic Books.

Gleick, J. (1987). *Chaos: Making a new science.* New York: Penguin Books.

Goldberg, Elkhonon (2001). *The executive brain: Frontal lobes and the civilized mind.* New York: Oxford University Press.

Goldberg, P. (1983). *The intuitive edge: Understanding and developing intuition.* Los Angeles: Jeremy Tarcher.

Goleman, D. (1995). *Emotional intelligence.* New York: Bantam Books.

Goodlad, J. (1984). *A place called school: Prospects for the future.* New York: McGraw-Hill.

Gopnik, A., Meltzoff, A. N., & Kuhl, P. K. (1999). *The scientist in the crib: Minds, brains, and how children learn.* New York: William Morrow.

Gould, S. J. (1996). *The mismeasure of man.* New York: W. W. Norton.

Graham, J. (1997). *The errancy: Poems.* Hopewell, NJ: Ecco Press.

Greene, M. (1992). Texts and Margins. In M. R. Goldberg and A. Phillips (Eds.), *Arts as education.* Cambridge, MA: Harvard Educational Review. Reprint Series, No. 24.

Greenspan, S. I., & Benderly, B. L. (1997). *The growth of the mind and the endangered origins of intelligence.* Reading, MA: Perseus Books.

Hart, L. (1983). *Human brain, human learning.* Oak Creek, AZ: Books for Educators.

Hayes-Jacob, H. (1989). *Interdisciplinary curriculum: Design and implementation.* Alexandria, VA: Association for Curriculum Development.

Healy, J. (1994). *Your child's growing mind.* New York: Doubleday.

James, W. (1956). *The will to believe.* New York: Dover Publications.

James, W. (1958). *Talks to teachers.* New York: W. W. Norton.

Jung, C. (1976). *Psychological types.* New Jersey: Princeton University Press.

Kallick, B., & Costa, A. (1991). Through the lens of a critical friend. In *Educational leadership.* Alexandria, VA: Association for Curriculum Development.

Kegan, R. (1982). *The evolving self: Problems and process in human development.* Cambridge, MA: Harvard University Press.

Kolb, D. A. (1983). *Experiential learning: Experience as the source of learning and development.* Englewood Cliffs, NJ: Prentice Hall.

LeDoux, J. (1996). *The emotional brain: The mysterious underpinnings of emotional life.* New York: Simon & Schuster.

Lewin, K. (1951). *Field theory in social sciences.* New York: Harper & Row.

Luria, A. (1980). *Higher cortical functions in man* (2nd ed.). New York: Basic Books.

Machado, L. A. (1980). *The right to be intelligent.* New York: Pergamon Press.

McCarthy, B. (1996). *About learning.* Wauconda, IL: About Learning, Inc.

McCarthy, B., & Morris, S. (1999). *4MAT in action: Lesson units for all grades* (4th ed.). Wauconda, IL: About Learning, Inc.

McCarthy, D. (2000). *4MATION software.* Wauconda, IL: About Learning, Inc.

McGaugh, J. L. (1992). Affect, neuromodulatory systems, and memory storage. In S.-A. Christianson (Ed.), *The handbook of emotion and memory: Research and theory.* Hillsdale, NJ: Lawrence Erlbaum.

McGinn, C. (1999). *The mysterious flame: Conscious minds in a material world.* New York: Basic Books.

Musick, M. (1996). *Setting education standards high enough.* Atlanta, GA: Southern Regional Education Board.

Noddings, N., & Shore, P. J. (1984). *Awakening the inner eye: Intuition in education.* New York: Columbia Teachers College Press.

Oliver, M. (1998). *Rules for the dance.* Boston: Houghton Mifflin.

Ornstein, R. (1997). *The right mind: Making sense of the hemispheres.* New York: Harcourt Brace.

Perrone, V. (1991). Toward more powerful assessment. educational leadership. In *Expanding student assessment.* Alexandria, VA: Association for Curriculum Development.

Piaget, J. (1990). *Child's perception of the world.* New York: Basic Books, 1929, Reprint.

Popham, W. J. (1999). *Classroom assessment: What teachers need to know* (2nd ed.). Boston: Allyn and Bacon.

Ramachandran, V. S., & Blakeslee, S. (1998). *Phantoms in the brain: Probing the mysteries of the human mind.* New York: William Morrow.

Resnick, L. (1987). *Education and learning to think.* Washington, DC: National Research Council.

Restak, R. (1990). *The modular brain.* New York: Simon & Schuster.

Restak, R. (1991). *The brain has a mind of its own: Insights from a practicing neurologist.* New York: Harmony Books.

Rutherford, F. J., & Ahlgren, A. (1990). *Science for all Americans.* New York: Oxford University Press.

Sanders, J., & Sanders, D. (1984). *Teaching creativity through metaphor.* New York: Longman.

Schacter, D. (1996). *Searching for memory: The brain, the mind, and the past.* New York: Basic Books.

Senge, P. M., Kliener, A., Roberts, C., Ross, R. B., & Smith, B. J. (1994). *The fifth discipline field book: Strategies and tools for building a learning organization.* New York: Doubleday.

Shlain, L. (1998). *The alphabet versus the goddess: The conflict between word and image.* New York: Viking.

Siegel, D. (1999). *The developing mind: Toward a neurobiology of interpersonal experience.* New York: Guilford Press.

Storr, A. (1992). *Music and the mind.* New York: Free Press.

Tarrant, J. (1998). *The light inside the dark: Zen, soul and the spiritual life.* New York: HarperCollins.

TenHouten, W. D. (1985). Cerebral-lateralization theory and the sociology of knowledge in the dual brain. In D. F. Benson and E. Zaidel (Eds.), *Brain: Hemispheric specialization in humans.* New York: Guilford Press.

Tucker, M., & Codding, J. (1998). *Standards for our schools: How to set them, measure them, and reach them.* San Francisco: Jossey-Bass.

Vygotsky, L. S. (1978). *Mind in society: The development of higher psychological processes.* Cambridge, MA: Harvard University Press.

West, T. G. (1991). *In the mind's eye: Visual thinkers, gifted people with learning difficulties, computer images, and the ironies of creativity.* Buffalo, NY: Prometheus Books.

Westcott, M., & Ranzoni, J. (1963). Correlates of intuitive thinking. *Psychological Reports, 12,* 595–613.

Whyte, D. (1996). *The heart aroused: Poetry and the preservation of the soul in corporate America.* New York: Doubleday.

Wiggins, G. P. (1993). *Assessing student performance: Exploring the purpose and limits of testing.* San Francisco: Jossey-Bass.

Zull, James. (2002). *The art of changing the brain: Enriching teaching by exploring the biology of learning.* Sterling, VA: Stylus Publishing.

Index